Strange Happenings in
CORNWALL

Michael Williams

Bossiney Books

First published in 1981
by Bossiney Books
St Teath, Bodmin, Cornwall
Designed, Typeset and printed in Great Britain by
Penwell Ltd., Parkwood, Callington
Cornwall

PLATE ACKNOWLEDGEMENTS

Cover photograph by Ray Bishop
Pages 13, 14, 37, 76, 80, The Woolf Greenham Collection
Pages 5, 21, 31, 33, 38, 45, 49, 52, 56, 57, 65, 71,
78, 79, 90, 93, Ray Bishop
Pages 59, 62, Ray Bishop, by courtesy of Hall of Chivalry
Page 26 Reg Watkiss, by courtesy of Denis Mitchell
Pages 7, 22 David Clarke
Page 25 Andrew Lanyon
Page 35 Kensington Library
Page 50 Ronald Youlton
Page 9 Peter Dryden
Page 11 David and Joan Wills
Page 66 Peter Keeling
Page 88 Vic Roberts

ABOUT THE AUTHOR

A Cornishman, Michael Williams started full time publishing in 1975. With his wife Sonia, he runs Bossiney Books from a cottage and converted barn in North Cornwall — they are literally Cornish cottage publishers, specializing in Westcountry subjects by Westcountry authors.

For ten years they ran the Bossiney House Hotel, just outside Tintagel — hence the name Bossiney Books. Then in 1975 they left the hotel business and moved to St Teath. This is their seventy-first title.

The author of ten books, Michael Williams says: 'I enjoy this way of life immensely, publishing full-time and promoting the work of our writers, and still managing to find time to do a book of my own now and then. It's hard work, very challenging but very fulfilling.'

Strange shapes and strange characters, healing and life after death, reincarnation and Spiritualism, murders and mysteries are only some of the contents in this fascinating book about *Strange Happenings in Cornwall*. There is also a chapter on the night that frightened Cornwall. 'My interview with someone who claims to have been King Arthur in an earlier life,' says Michael Williams, 'was an incredible experience. And, of course, the whole subject of Arthur and Cornwall could now take on a new meaning.' A book that is destined to entertain and enlighten, to be applauded and to be attacked.

Strange Happenings in Cornwall

'Cornwall works on me. Take this one valley here. If I stayed here a hundred years I shouldn't have exhausted its painting possibilities. Maybe it's just because I am a Cornishman, but you get this feeling of place.'

That's what the Cornish painter Dick Gilbert told me when we talked in a valley near Ludgvan fifteen years ago.

I now know what he means.

When I wrote *Cornish Mysteries* back in 1980, I was on a kind of second innings, writing in the wake of my earlier *Supernatural in Cornwall,* and now at the beginning of a third exploration among strange happenings, I find the possibilities are still there: one project invariably leading to something else.

On these three Cornish journeys I have frequently remembered some words of Lady Clara Vyvyan's. Of the Cornish atmosphere she once said: 'It never beckons you on and on with unfulfilled promise. All the time it is close to you . . . a peculiar intimacy between man and nature . . .' How right she was. Time and time again the Supernatural or the strange — or both — have signposted the way.

Cornwall has probably had more than her share of strange happenings. The remoteness of the region, the nature of the land and seascapes, the character of the people — all these are factors but it is just impossible to put your finger on one simple explanation or a neat combination of reasons.

Maybe the Cornish people come into all this. Perhaps many of us live in the past as well as the present. I cannot, say, walk across

'I cannot walk across those bleached grasses of Bodmin Moor, the wind in my face, and not feel somehow related to earlier events.' ▶

those bleached grasses of Bodmin Moor, the wind in my face, and not feel somehow related to earlier events. I cannot stand amid the Hurlers near Minions and divorce past from present. Handling one of those beautiful grey stones generates the notion that you're in touch with a distant people — and power.

Rosalie Glyn Grylls, in the now sadly extinct *Cornish Review,* pinned the Cornish character to paper brilliantly. 'The first thing about the Cornish,' she wrote, 'is that they are not nice: exciting and attractive but not nice. They have colour enough to turn the spectacles of most onlookers pink but it is not fast to light. The impulsiveness that goes as far as magnanimity does not sustain generosity; the devotion, loyal for fanaticism, has no fidelity; the forthcomingness keeps much more back than reticence — like an iceberg two thirds under the water, if there were not anything less like an ice-berg than any Celt . . . Where does it go, then, all the colour? The warm tones of manner, the light and shade of speech? The colour goes into the personality. Almost one might say it is not enough for the Cornish to be Cornish; but not quite for they have a full measure of Celtic discontent. The energy that makes for colourfulness goes into the business of living — always a hard one in Cornwall — the fervour into congregational worship, into a personal relationship with omnipotence not into embellishing its dwellingplace; the enterprise into seeking fortunes afield.'

A few words of warning, however, before we begin journeying across Cornwall in search of the strange and often the inexplicable. Cornish housewives are by no means in 100 per cent agreement about the correct ingredients of the Cornish pasty, and I suspect there will be disagreement about some of the contents in this book.

I doubt, for example, whether Alan Nance would consider either Spiritualism or healing as remotely strange. But for many both are something of a mystery. The convinced reincarnationist will not find it strange that people, living in the Westcountry today, were also here in King Arthur's reign. As the late and controversial Professor Joad would have said 'It all depends . . .'

Some of these stories have a strong Supernatural flavour. Others have none whatsoever. But I believe the majority of people will find them strange — and compelling.

'. . . a peculiar intimacy between man and nature . . .' ▶

Strange Shapes

There are many strange shapes in the Cornish landscape and I decided to do a tour of some of them. St Ives happens to be one of my favourite Cornish towns — so where better to begin such a journey?

Cornwall has some strange ceremonies too — and there are few odder than an event that takes place high above the town once every five years.

The high ground in the direction of Halsetown is full of atmosphere and stark beauty. Sir Henry Irving, the first Knight of the British theatre, spent part of his boyhood hereabouts. 'A wild and weird place,' he later reflected, 'fascinating in its own peculiar beauty, and taking more definite shape in my youthful imagination by reason of the fancies and legends of the people. The stories attaching to rock and well and hill are unending, every man and woman had folklore to tell us youngsters. We took them naturally — they seem to fit in wisely with the solitudes, the expanses, the superstitious nature of the Cornish people.'

Did they tell the boy Henry Irving about Mayor Knill and his curious legacy? He may even have seen this odd bit of Cornish 'theatre' that belongs to St Ives.

The Knill Monument, above Halsetown, is near the once-famed St Ives Consol Mines. Knill is its name because the idea was conceived by John Knill, a colourful enigmatic Cornishman. Born in Callington, Knill worked as an attorney's clerk in Penzance and then went to London. However, like many Cornishmen seeking fame in the capital, he came back to Cornwall, returning as the political

'If the ghost of John Knill haunts this windswept spot, does he chuckle?' ▶

agent of the Earl of Buckinghamshire in St Ives. For twenty years — from 1762 — Knill was Collector of Taxes and yet surprisingly he remained a popular figure in St Ives society. Moreover he was so good at his job that he was sent to the West Indies, at one stage, to advise on reorganizing the West Indian method of collecting taxes.

On coming back to St Ives, Knill became the owner of a privateer. Until about 1815, most people of substance in the town invested in privateers. These vessels, licensed by the Government, were entitled to attack enemy ships, and it became a lucrative business because though cargoes, according to the letter of the Law, were subject to Duty, this was often avoided. The numerous vaults and subterranean passages — not to mention the strong local smuggling tradition — all combined to help in evading Duty.

Knill's house stands to this day, still recognisable in narrow Fore Street, but the man will always be best remembered for his surprising and puzzling steeple. This granite pyramid, on a high hill south-east of the town, can be seen for miles around. Surrounded by a cluster of rhododendrons and bearing the Knill family coat of arms, it was constructed in 1782. Mayor Knill planned to lie in his granite mausoleum, but circumstances torpedoed his intention. Soon after the Steeple was built, Knill, following his first profession, the Law, returned once more to London and he died there. So instead of resting here at St Ives, his bones lie in St Andrew's Church, Holborn.

However, once every five years, John Knill is remembered in extraordinary style in his native Cornwall. Twice in a decade on St James's Day a strange ceremony takes place here at the Steeple.

The trustees of this unusual property were the Vicar of St Ives, the Mayor of St Ives and the local Collector of Customs. St Ives no longer has its Collector of Customs, but the other two trustees ensure that Knill's eccentric wish is carried out every five years. The custom — perhaps Pagan — is that ten small girls and two widows, with a fiddler to lead them, dance to the 'folly' on the appointed day, dance there for at least a quarter of an hour, sing *All People that on Earth do Dwell,* and then return to the town. Moreover they get paid for the performance. John Knill's instructions were that £10 should be shared among the girls, each widow should receive £2, and the fiddler be paid £1 for his music-making — while the trustees should be granted the sum of £10 to entertain two guests each to dinner — a generous sum perhaps in 1801.

10

If the ghost of John Knill haunts this windswept spot, does he chuckle? Did he laugh to himself when, in person, he attended the first ceremony in 1801? Did he really intend to use this Steeple as his mausoleum? Or was it a Daymark to help the Privateers coming into the lovely sweep of St Ives Bay?

Maybe both. But we shall never know for sure.

From St Ives I took that beautiful twisting coastal road, via Zennor, for St Just. My next destination among the strange shapes was the Tregeseal Stone Circle. This ancient colony stands below the Hooting Carn. History can, in fact, tell us next to nothing about these circles that mysteriously people the British landscape. Man's records do not reach beyond the first daylight of civilisation — and yet there was twilight of something earlier — and here we enter a field of speculation.

These stones at Tregeseal then remain a fascinating riddle. Men and women have offered all sorts of theories — monuments or temples or areas for astronomers, these are just some of the ideas put forward — but as these stones weather against the seasons, so

'These stones at Tregeseal then remain a fascinating riddle . . . they defy human explanation.'

they defy human explanation. Walking inside and around them generated a curious primitive thrill. Touching them I felt, in some mystical way, that I was in touch with the 'old people'.

Now the cynic may scoff, muttering about the power of auto-suggestion. But I decline to take such a Doubting Thomas view. T.C. Lethbridge, the well-known archaeologist and psychic researcher, in an effort to date another Cornish circle, the Merry Maidens, also in Penwith, had a strange experience.

In his book *The Legend of the Suns of God*, he recalled that experience near Lamorna: 'As soon as the pendulum started to swing, a strange thing happened. The hand resting on the stones received a strong tingling sensation like a mild electric shock and the pendulum itself shot out until it was circling nearly horizontally to the ground. The stone itself, which must have weighed over a ton, felt as if it were rocking and almost dancing about. This was quite alarming, but I stuck to my counting . . . The next day I sent my wife up along to see what happened to her. She had the same experience. It has happened nowhere else. The Pipers were mute and so were many crosses and other monuments which I have tried. But most circular monuments are now incomplete and perhaps something has gone from them.'

Someone else who has experienced the power of ancient stones is fellow Bossiney author Joan Rendell. She told me recently, 'I had a strange experience at an ancient burial ground at Cashtal Yn Ard, a Neolithic burial place on the Isle of Man. This was where chieftains were buried in the New Stone Age, about 2000 BC. When two friends and I visited the site I felt a very strong "atmosphere" there and when I placed the palms of my hands against one of the upright stones still remaining from the megalithic chambered cairn I exclaimed "Oh, I can feel the vibrations". My friends were overcome with mirth at this revelation and so I did not press the point but I could quite definitely feel a tingling sensation going right through my body. I have since discovered that the higher up the stone one touches the stronger the vibrations become.'

The fogou at Rosemerryn: 'The fogou for me had a more holy air than many churches.' ▶

My exploration among the strange shapes now took me to a third destination in the Hundred of Penwith, to the Parish of St Buryan.

Rosemerryn stands at the head of the lovely Lamorna Valley, the house and cottage occupying the site of a two-thousand-year-old hill-fort. There were three good reasons for my visit: to meet the owner, Jo May, a psychologist, and visit the house and fogou.

This time I was meeting my first fogou. These strange underground structures have baffled historians and scholars for a long, long time. Their true purpose remains a complete Cornish mystery. Storage has been a recurring suggestion, but the deeper more specific solution has remained elusive. Their dates — certain dates anyway — are lost in the mists of distant history, and for all the careful scholarly investigation they remain objects of speculation.

Back in Plymouth, some time ago, in Barney Camfield's home, where much healing work is done, I encountered an atmosphere of great peace and power and the same quality hung in the air at Lamorna. Jo May told me how he often brought his groups here for meditation. 'The results of meditation are good in the fogou, and we have even had people who have heard music. A well-travelled psychic told me she had only met such a healing atmosphere in the Red Indian reservations in the States.

Rosemerryn is, in fact, the base for a group called CAER — Centre for Alternative Education and Research — the title interestingly coming from the Cornish word *Caer,* meaning 'Fort'. Jo May, who is its director, runs groups and workshops covering many areas including relationships, encounter, transpersonal psychology, yoga, wholefood cooking and self-sufficiency.

'We believe that the peaceful and magical atmosphere is especially conducive to group work and the developing of trust. Though my wife and I have parted since coming here, we remain good friends, and in any case we were drifting apart before that, so Rosemerryn even worked very constructively in that sense.'

'Psychics have studied the fogou and the feeling is that it was used for birth, death and rebirth, and almost certainly overseen by women.'

◀'Jo May is quite sure the fogou is an accumulator for earth force . . . different people have responded differently . . .'

The fogou, for me, had a more holy air than many churches. Some old buildings have a dead quality, yet curiously inside these stone walls I felt I was standing in a living presence. I can honestly say I came back out into the sunlight feeling better, refreshed and renewed.

Jo May is quite sure the fogou is an accumulator for earth force. Interestingly different people have responded differently: some people have felt nausea, others have experienced vivid imagery; while dowsing has produced a reaction, indicating an energy field some fifteen feet wide running along the fogou's path.

If ever there was a curse on this place, I felt very strongly it had gone. If witchcraft had ever left a lingering something that too had gone. The stones had a good feel. The religious atmosphere is heightened by the presence of a carving 'depicting a healing entity or spirit'.

There are other religious hints about the fogou. The extremity has been shaped into a curve with a step and shelving — a shrine conceivably? At the far end of the 'creep' — a hidden chamber — a large stone blocks what appears to be a second entrance — a secret one for 'initiates'?

The house of Rosemerryn has a genuinely haunted reputation. Many local folk, especially in earlier generations, believed the place had been 'cursed' because people, involved with the house, had died either early or strangely — and sometimes both.

Rosemerryn was, in fact, the home of the Cornish writer Crosbie Garstin whose end was truly mysterious. In this lovely old house he worked at tremendous pressure to complete his last novel. He was desperately keen to finish the manuscript so that he could go with the Holman family on a yachting trip. Typing finished and manuscript posted to his London publisher, Garstin went on the trip — but never came back to Rosemerryn. One night at Salcombe in the process of saving a young girl from drowning, he lost his own life. Drama and mystery surrounded the whole episode in that his body was never found.

At the time some people thought Garstin had vanished into thin

Crosbie Garstin: '. . . in the process of saving a young girl from drowning, he lost his own life. Drama and mystery surrounded the whole episode . . .' ▶

air — to make a new start elsewhere. Others later saw an uncanny prophecy is his last paragraph, written probably only hours or, at most, days before his death and disappearance. In the Epilogue of that last published novel he wrote: 'Anthony Penhale sat motionless for a long while in thought. Then rising, he kissed the happy face and went downstairs to tell his wife that all was over — or all beginning.'

Was it all over? Or was there a new beginning?

We shall never know but it is just another mysterious facet in the life of this house.

Sitting in what was once Crosbie Garstin's old study, Jo May told me how others had come to sticky ends. The man, who had the house built in the first place, didn't live to enjoy it. Benjamin William Leader, the painter, was the first master of Rosemerryn. He had the house built in 1910 but he never came back from the Great War, having been killed in action. The male child of the house also died an unnatural death and Jo May's predecessor Tom Barneby, a botanist, was killed in a motoring accident. Jo May recalled how one local had told him soon after settling in Cornwall, 'I wouldn't live in *that* house and by that fogou!' Interestingly though Jo May has found that the house has created a positive atmosphere for his work.

'I first came to Rosemerryn to view the property, more than four years ago. Before I set foot inside the house I had this strong feeling as I walked around the grounds, "I must live here!" We did have some strange experiences to begin with . . . we heard this sad laughter of a woman. There were other ghostly phenomena: footsteps upstairs, footsteps that had no human rational explanation. There was the case too of a revolving bookcase that turned of its own accord, and outside in the grounds there was a six-barred gate which people would close every night, but *every* morning they would find it open.

'Since then things have settled down, and something seems to have been liberated. Personally, I feel no threat. Interestingly too neighbours reported a bad atmosphere until we came.'

As I drove back up the lane I had to remind myself Rosemerryn is probably one of the most haunted properties in all West Cornwall. Yet, on this sunlit June morning it seemed the happiest place in the world. I felt better for having come — and was sorry to leave.

★ ★ ★ ★ ★

My journey among the strange shapes now took me to the eastern flank of Bodmin Moor. Here in this magical landscape I visited one of the weirdest shapes in all Cornwall: the Cheesewring. It has the appearance of being man-made, the stones balancing beautifully on the western side of Stowe Hill, but the belief is it's a natural formation. Inevitably the Cheesewring is woven into Cornish folklore.

The legend is that this windswept spot was the home of a Druid who kept a cup of gold. The cup, whose contents were said to be inexhaustible, was regularly offered to any thirsty hunter who came this way, but one greedy hunter resolved to drink the cup dry. However, he failed to do just that. In an angry mood he rode off with the cup, but it was an ill-fated venture: his horse stumbled over rocks and the thieving huntsman was killed. The story goes that when he was buried, the cup too went into his moorland grave. Now that may seem just another weird and wonderful Cornish legend.

But there was an incredible sequel. Sometime in the 1830s a nearby barrow was opened — and inside they discovered a skeleton and, among the possessions, a ribbed gold cup! The kind that had been found in the tombs of the ancient Greeks, it was presented to King William IV. Alas His Majesty had little archaeological appreciation because after his death it was found in the Royal bathroom where the eccentric William had been using it as a shaving mug. Today the Rillaton Cup — as it is known — is housed in the British Museum, but a replica remains here in Cornwall: at the County Museum, Truro.

I came to the Cheesewring on a July morning, a day that might have been borrowed from autumn or winter, clouds racing across a stormy sky and the air that of mountains: cold and pure. From high ground, such as this, with the landscape stretching out below like a living map, you realise that Cornwall is a draughtsman's country. There is a sense of geometry in the terrain. I never come on to the Moorland without thinking of the painter Charles Simpson. It was he who first opened my eyes to the beauty and the magic of the Moors. 'There is an atmosphere of age in Cornwall,' he told me, 'and the early history of man seems to brood over these hills and moors . . .'

Standing in front of the Cheesewring you understand that Nature is a genius in sculpture. Richard Isbell, a friend who came with me on this exploration, handled the smooth surface of these stones. 'You'd think someone *must* have built these stones into these shapes,' he said. And he's right, for some of them are fashioned like furniture for a giant's hall. Up here, too, the silence is something very positive. I felt also that the primitive people were right to hold their religious ceremonies on high ground. There is something uplifting in the atmosphere. We agreed we both felt better for being there.

I rate the Cheesewring and Bowerman's Nose on Dartmoor as close relations and there *is* an interesting link. Some people thought these strange stone structures were the remains of huge interconnected power-storage temples, the Cornish temples being dedicated to the well-being of the body whereas their Devon counterparts were for revitalizing the spirit.

Intriguingly, too, the Cheesewring is part of a celebrated ley line, starting in Cornwall and ending in East Anglia. Janet and Colin Bord in their fascinating book *Mysterious Britain* devoted a chapter to Trackways & Leys: The Unseen Power.

'The basis of the ley system,' they wrote, 'is quite simple — that sites of ancient importance align. To test the theory use any Ordnance Survey maps — except of a "built-up" or mountainous area — scale 1 inch to 1 mile, and a perspex straight edge. Choose an area of the map and circle the following types of site: stone circles, standing stones, barrows, tumuli, "castles", motes and baileys, notes, hillforts, earthworks, churches, abbeys and other religious buildings; in fact anything which is very old or traditionally sacred — and then try and align some of them along the straight-edge. You will soon find many three-, four- and even five-point alignments, perhaps also six-, seven- and eight-point ones. In order to rule out coincidence, "ley hunters" stipulate that an alignment which merits further investigation must have at least five valid points aligning within a fairly short distance, that is ten rather than fifty miles . . .

'Although the existence of leys has been proved many times over, their real purpose is still uncertain. Alfred Watkins believed that they were early man's trackways . . . Later researchers believe that this is only part of the answer, and that the leys may in fact follow invisible lines of power criss-crossing the countryside. Early man

The Cheesewring on Bodmin Moor: 'Nature is a genius in sculpture . . . Up here, too, the silence is something very positive.' ▶

was aware of this power, which he harnessed for his own spiritual and physical benefit by erecting his "temples" at certain significant points along the power-lines . . . It is thought by some people that leys are used, possibly as a power source or navigational aid, by flying saucers or UFOs as they move around our skies.'

This particular ley line begins at St Michael's Mount, just off the Cornish coast in Mount's Bay, travels through to the Cheesewring here on Bodmin Moor, on to St Michael's Church at Brentor, up to Somerset to Burrow Mump and Glastonbury, on to Avebury in Wiltshire, further eastward following the approximate course of the Icknield Way, through Bury St Edmunds and finally crossing the coast north of Lowestoft. Or is it finally?

The fact is when you stand at the Cheesewring you are on a mysterious route, in an area of fascinating speculation. Either way, on a crystal-clear day you can enjoy marvellous views from Stowe Hill over the Tamar Valley to the east and out upon the brooding moors to the west.

◀ 'This particular ley line begins at St Michael's Mount . . .'

Strange Characters

From strange shapes to strange characters: we go back to St Ives, to a cottage in Back Road West.

The story of Alfred Wallis is not of rags to riches, but of a marine rag and bone merchant achieving belated eccentric fame as an artist.

Today St Ives is the art capital of Cornwall; times were though when the artist was viewed with suspicion. In the pioneering days, Louis Grier went down to the pier, one *Sunday* morning, to start painting, only to be told if he appeared there again 'on the Lord's Day' he, paints, brushes and easel, the lot would be flung into the water. I also heard the tale of a fish cart being driven up the steep slope of Skidden Hill, the pony jibbing and the driver ending a string of colourful abuse about the poor animal with the words 'You . . . you bloody artist?'

Wallis was born on the other side of the Tamar at Devonport in 1855. The family was poor, and he probably never went to school. Wallis says he went to sea as a cabin boy when only nine years old, and that he spent sixteen tough years sailing to and fro across the Atlantic in schooners, windjammers and 'Cod Bankers' to Newfoundland. But there are people in St Ives who believe he never went to sea; while a step-grandson claimed, 'I don't think he could stand the sea!' — and that is only part of the enigma.

At the age of twenty at Penzance, he married Susan Ward, a widow many years his senior and the mother of seventeen children. Susan gave birth to two children of Wallis's but both died young. Then in 1890 they left Penzance and settled in St Ives, first at Bethesada Hill, and then moving, as his rag and bone business grew, down on to the famous St Ives harbour front. Travelling around the narrow streets, asking for scrap metal, Wallis acquired the nickname 'Old Iron' and St Ives gossip has it that children

**Alfred Wallis's rag and bone store at St Ives:
'Wallis acquired the nick name "Old Iron".'**

would sell him some scrap for a penny or two, then promptly nick it from the back of the cart and sell it to him a second time!

Despite the alleged pilfering, the business must have prospered because in 1912, at the age of 56, he was able to buy the cottage in Back Road West — Number 3 — and retire. He did some odd jobs after the move, helping a local antique dealer and doing some labouring work during the war. He also achieved a kind of trading fame, becoming the first man to make and sell ice cream in the streets of St Ives.

In June 1922 Susan died, and this proved to be a crucial turning point in his life. At the age of seventy, he began to paint 'for company'. He was now a lonely man, not caring for St Ives society, and, without art training of any kind, started painting prolifically. Through Susan's death a primitive painter of originality was born. Childlike paintings began to appear on scraps of card and old canvases or even odd bits of paper: ships and houses, lighthouses and cottages but ships and the sea were his constantly recurring theme.

The sea was clearly the window of his world, and many of his

This painting by Alfred Wallis
was the first one that Ben
Nicholson bought when he went
to St Ives for the day with
Christopher Wood in August
1928: 'This was an exciting day,
for not only was it the first time
I saw St Ives but on the way
back from Porthmeor Beach we
passed an open door in Back
Road West and through it saw
some paintings of ships and
houses on odd pieces of paper
and cardboard nailed up all over
the walls, with particularly large
nails through the smallest ones.
We knocked on the door and
inside found Wallis and the
paintings we got from him were
the first he made.'
(Ben Nicholson, *Horizon,* 1943)

paintings have an intensity that tells us he was more than an old man doodling with paints as compensation for lack of companionship. It's interesting to speculate why he used so few colours. His pictures rarely got beyond dark brown and black, grey and white, and that strong green which is somehow peculiar to Cornwall and things Cornish. Curious too that St Ives should have produced another primitive painter in the Wallis mould in recent years in the person of Bryan Pearce.

Kathleen Watkins, Curator of the Penwith Gallery, told me, 'Looking out to sea from above Porthminster I can often see an Alfred Wallis sea . . . the colours are right from his paintings . . . it's just an Alfred Wallis sea.' The Penwith Gallery appropriately staged the first major Alfred Wallis exhibition in 1968, just a hundred metres from his old cottage. Kathleen Watkins recalls, 'The exhibition was very well received by the present-day painters.'

Alan Bowness, writing an introduction to the catalogue for that exhibition, which also went to the Tate Gallery in London, thought Wallis 'close in spirit to certain medieval and early Renaissance artists. I think of him like some old monk, working in his cell, reading his Bible when he was not painting. And if instead of illustrating stories from the Bible or the lives of the saints, Wallis preferred a clear, unsentimental, childlike view of life as he had known it, there is nevertheless a certain feeling of a paradise that is lost and to be regained in heaven.'

Rarely leaving his cottage, Alfred Wallis once wrote: 'What I do mosley is what use To Bee out of my own memery . . .' Some people thought him 'not exactly right in the head' and others maintained, 'He could hear the Devil . . . the Devil was always upstairs.' He had joined the Salvation Army back in 1904, and held austere convictions. But there was little of the brotherhood spirit about him in his advancing years. He lived like a hermit and became a legend in his strange lifetime in Back Road West, his deafness intensifying his sense of isolation. A gnome-like figure in his fisherman's jersey, he was little more than five feet in height, and prone to rages. He believed he'd been cheated out of an Australian legacy as a young man, so there'd always been a sizeable chip on his shoulder and as he grew older a persecution complex deepened. In his last years he became convinced evil spirits were being sent to his cottage to torment him.

I have stood outside his old cottage and wondered what he would have made of his considerable reputation today — though many argue as to just how good or great he was. Maybe it is something he would have ignored — or would this semi-illiterate character have failed to grasp all the implications? Apparently he sold many of his paintings for next to nothing and gave a good many away. I have also stood in front of his work at the Penwith Gallery and tried to make up my mind whether his pictures were an old fisherman remembering — or a rag and bone merchant looking out to sea, safely from the mainland.

An August day in 1928 proved to be another important date for Wallis. On that day two professional artists, Ben Nicholson and Kit Wood, walking back from Porthmeor Beach, passing the open door of Number 3 Back Road West saw a few of his paintings and bought some. Wallis, though, had made more than 'sales', he had been 'discovered'. Thanks to Nicholson's interest and influence, Wallis became the centre of a circle of admirers and patrons, influential ones too, people like H.S. Ede at the Tate, Sir Herbert Read, Adrian Stokes, the potter Bernard Leach and the Cornish painter Peter Lanyon. But no more than thirty people took a genuine interest in Wallis's work in his lifetime.

Was it all a put-up job then? Some people thought so — and still do.

Edwin Mullins, Wallis's biographer, touched on this subject: '. . . people to whom it never occurred to take seriously an old rag-and-bone man who doodled with paints in his dotage. Now they are reluctantly compelled to take him seriously, if only because he has appeared in the colour supplements, and because they know his paintings fetch high prices in London galleries. Time and again a rueful voice has told me, "I could 'ave 'ad 'undreds ob'm, and I'd be rich now".

'The people in St Ives who are doubly irritated by his posthumous success are those who in the 1930s were proud that the town should be attracting successful and respectable painters from London to work there, and who were proud to patronise them. The collections such people formed are now substantially worthless as the great academic names of the day are forgotten. Wallis was the one man whose work they never thought of buying. The situation is not unlike that of a loyal servant who reads one morning that his master has left all his possessions to the mongrel dog.

'Wallis's success has therefore engendered some irritation in St

Ives and there is many a true Cornishman who firmly believes it is all a put-up job and an affront to local pride. One elderly pillar of local trade expressed this view to me unequivocally on his doorstep one day. "Wallis," he growled, "Wallis; a lot of childish trash worked up into something like the Beatles by publicity." '

The last days of Wallis's life read like a tragedy. He had a dread — shared by many of his class and generation — of ending his days in a workhouse, and that alas was his fate. Sick and no longer able to fend for himself, he was despatched to Madron Workhouse in June 1941, and died there in the August of the following year. People, like Ben Nicholson and Adrian Stokes, generously saw to it that he had painting materials in the last months of his life at Madron, but the old man's sight was fading and his hand had grown shaky. It is good to know though that he kept on painting until the end.

And the same friends, who had been generous in his lifetime, rallied again in death, financing the arrangements for his funeral, and saving him the indignity of a pauper's grave.

They brought him 'home', back to St Ives for a Salvation Army funeral, and buried him in Porthmeor Cemetery. His grave is a slab covered with tiles, shaped by the potter Bernard Leach, in the form of a lighthouse. The inscription consists of just five words: 'Alfred Wallis, Artist and Mariner.'

As with Mayor John Knill, I wonder if there is a ghostly chuckle.

After the painter's death, the St Ives authorities came close to creating a Gilbert and Sullivan situation by insisting on burning the contents of Wallis's cottage, including something like a hundred of his paintings. Fortunately Adrian Stokes convinced them the scraps of painted cardboard were of *some* value, and braving filth and fleas he rescued them.

I never come along Back Road West without thinking of him. Coming to life as a painter in his seventies, when most men have put their feet up, he created original memorable art out of the chaos of old age, loneliness and persecution. Applauded by some, rejected by others, the life and work of Alfred Wallis are extraordinary: a strange Westcountryman indeed.

★ ★ ★ ★ ★

To travel from St Ives to Truro is to move from one Cornish society to another and to move from Alfred Wallis to John Wolcot is to study eccentricity in extremes.

'Old, obscene, beastly Peter Pindar,' Charles Lamb called him. Coleridge agreed: 'I swear to you that my flesh creeps at his name!' And de Quincey dismissed him as 'that buffoon . . .' But Wordsworth put him on quite another level: 'Boileau and Pope and the redoubted Peter. These are great names.' While Robert Burns declared: 'A delightful fellow and a first favourite of mine.'

John Wolcot, alias Peter Pindar, lived outside the pages of fiction, but proved the old cliché right — fact is often stranger. He was born in Devon in 1738, the second son of a surgeon, but an air of mystery surrounds his first day in this world — nobody bothered to record his birthday. When his father died in 1751, he was despatched to Cornwall, to Fowey, where he was brought up by two strict aunts. He received an important slice of his education at Bodmin Grammar School and became a protégé of Sir William Trelawney of Trelawne. This was a fated event for the young man as, when he qualified at Aberdeen, Sir William, then Governor, took him to Jamaica as his physician.

In her book *Opie and His Circle,* Ada Earland gave us this picture of the young Westcountryman: '. . . a good boon companion, able to tell a coarse story with the best, witty, well read, musical, a good amateur artist — able to divert Sir William, or drive away the ennui from Lady Trelawney, as required. No Saint, we may be sure, and yet a man with much good in him.'

He was all that: a poet, political satirist, journalist too, and improbably a parson. Physician-General in Jamaica, he was ordained in 1769, surely one of the strangest shepherds in the Church of England's history. Three years later Sir William died and Jamaican gossip had it that he would marry Sir William's widow. But he did not. He came back to Cornwall, to the Cathedral City of Truro, obtaining a house from Mr Daniell and setting up a medical practice in what today is The Britannia.

The Reverend Richard Polwhele referred to him as 'a good doctor, but a bad man'. Nevertheless he proceeded to build a big and successful practice. Fellow physicians, though, disliked his unortho-

'John Wolcot, alias Peter Pindar, lived outside the
pages of fiction, but proved the old cliché right
— fact is often stranger.' (Painting by Opie) ▶

doxy. On one occasion a patient, a lady, was suffering from a fever. Crisis point was reached and Wolcot prescribed lobster. Only a putrid lobster on a dung heap could be found, but the Doctor insisted that the vile remnant be taken to his patient. She revived instantly!

This man, with two names (he wrote under the name of Peter Pindar) and several talents is not only one of the strangest characters in Westcountry history, but also an important impressario. Without John Wolcot, the odds are we should never have heard of the Cornish painter John Opie.

One day on a call to the Nankivell family at Mithian John Wolcot saw a painting of Mrs Nankivell's cat, painted by an uncouth fifteen-year-old Opie. The Doctor sensed he had come across a prodigy of considerable talent. In conversation, Mrs Nankivell mentioned the lad's talents in paint, and Wolcot was keen to meet him and see more of his work.

Wolcot found the lad working in the sawpit. 'How do you like painting?' he asked.

'Better than my bread and meat,' was Opie's reply.

The boy revered his mother. She had married Edward Opie, a mine carpenter of Mithian, who did not approve of young John's enthusiasm for art. He wanted to thrash 'the artistic nonsense' out of the boy but Mary Opie came between father and son. 'The boy was good for naught,' Edward Opie complained, 'could never make a wheelbarrow, was always gazing upon cats and staring volks in the face.'

Mrs Opie too could well have been relieved when Wolcot bought her son out of his apprenticeship and took him to live with him at The Britannia. Some tension must have been taken from the family life.

There was, though, no hint of homosexuality. Wolcot was, in fact, a great womanizer. He spent a good deal of money entertaining ladies or paying prostitutes for sexual satisfaction. At one stage he proposed to a certain Truro lady, but she married someone else and caused a third man to shoot himself.

Wolcot became Opie's tutor in two senses: painter and gentleman. In the eighteenth century only a portrait painter had the chance of living by his brush. 'Look to originals!' the tutor urged. 'Stare volks in the face! Canvass 'em from top to toe, mark their features, air, manner, gesture, attitude!' In addition to running his practice and giving the boy art lessons, he introduced him to the Classics, music, the French language and society manners. In a letter the doctor wrote of his protégé: 'I want to polish him; he is an unlicked cub yet. I want to make him learn to respect himself.'

The doctor's must have been a busy life for, as Peter Pindar, his satirical verse was hitting many targets — the authorities at Truro were a frequent objective — but these literary exploits made him little money and numerous enemies.

Soon he launched John Opie on the career of travelling portrait painter, the boy setting out with letters of introduction and recommendation to the doctor's friends and patients. The best of his guinea portraits, painted between the age of sixteen and nineteen, rank among his most brilliant work.

The tide of opinion in Truro, nevertheless, was running against the doctor. He caused uproars at dinner parties, he continued to

The Britannia Inn, Truro: 'Wolcot bought her son out of his apprenticeship and took him to live with him at The Britannia.'

clash with the Corporation and his unconventional approach in medicine made him a despised figure within the profession. His practice, through it all, though, continued to flourish. But a move from Truro became almost inevitable, and he went westward to Helston, where he took up residence in Coinage Hall Street and practised between Helston and Falmouth. On a visit to Falmouth, Wolcot demonstrated considerable courage by blindfolding some horses and leading them from a blazing stable.

The practice of medicine, however, seemed to give him no deep personal satisfaction. He yearned for self-expression in paint and words. His departure in 1781 looked like a sudden decision, but Wolcot, seeing Opie as the means of his escape from medicine and himself as the young painter's impressario, had been scheming the move for some time.

He took his protégé to London, an act which some, on reflection, regarded as a misfortune.

The late Judge J.W. Scobell Armstrong, in a catalogue of the John Opie and Henry Bone Exhibition, organised by the Royal Institution of Cornwall in 1951, wrote:

'In the case of a precocious and impressionable lad, such as Opie then was, the plunge into an alien, uncongenial and confusing environment could hardly fail to impair his character, and contact with the "schools" under such conditions was unlikely to improve his painting. A "school", whether it be a school of painting or a school of poetry, always imparts into the pursuit of art those elements of imitation and rivalry, which only the strongest characters can escape, and it is greatly to Opie's credit that his genius survived such a test so little scathed.

'Wolcot, who was an artful advertiser, dressed his young protégé picturesquely, adorned his head with a green feather, and encouraged him to remain rough-mannered and uncouth. Those who visited the Orange Court in order to be painted by the "Cornish Wonder", were many of them fashionable nonentities. They treated the strangely attired young barbarian from Ultima Thale with an amused condescension, which he bitterly resented. Disliking them profoundly, he seldom regarded them as worth painting, and, since he did not possess sufficient imagination and insight to discern the soul that sometimes lurked behind an unpleasing and inexpressive countenance, he did not always do full justice to his sitters. The furrows that ravaged the faces of the old, the tenderness of

John Opie: 'There is a new genius . . . a
Cornish lad of nineteen, who has taught himself
to colour in a bold masterly style.'

maternity, the strong lineaments that denoted courage and intelligence, these he always painted faithfully . . .'

Opie's first year in London suggested great success. The wily Wolcot obtained an interview with George III, and the King's interest in the young Cornishman accelerated popularity. But such popularity declined in the second year. The fact is, Opie painted with absolute candour. He ignored human vanity. If dignity or beauty were discernible in the sitter, he painted the qualities faithfully. But if they were not in evidence, his pictures exposed such shortcomings with brutal clarity.

Horace Walpole noted this characteristic. In a letter, dated 14 February, 1782, he wrote:

'There is a new genius: one Opy, a Cornish lad of nineteen, who has taught himself to colour in a bold masterly style, by studying nature and painting from beggars and poor children. He has done a head of Mrs Delany for the King — Oui vraiment, it is pronounced like Rembrandt, but as I told her, it does not look older than she is, but older than she does.'

Another characteristic which counted against the painter was his sardonic humour. Once he was painting an old beau, who screwed up his mouth ridiculously . . . 'Sir,' he said, 'if you want the mouth left out, I will do it with pleasure!' On another occasion he was asked how he mixed his colours. His reply was typical: 'With brains, sir.' While on the subject of painting actors, he commented acidly: 'Confound them! They have everybodies' faces but their own. What can I make them?'

John Opie, to his credit, worked hard, educating himself. Apart from increasing his technical knowledge of painting, he read the best authors and sought the company of the cleverest men. He ultimately became an engaging conversationalist, terse and frank. Northcote described him as 'the greatest man who ever came under my observation — but I do not say the greatest painter . . .'

But in any analysis of Opie, there *must* be enormous debt to John Wolcot. Without Wolcot, fame and fortune are very likely to have eluded the young man.

In London, with Opie maturing, there were clashes between the two men. Cash flowed into the joint coffers, thanks to Wolcot's publicity work and Opie's painting, but Wolcot took more than his share, spending a good deal of it on whores.

It was in 1806 that Opie was elected Professor of Painting at the

Royal Academy, and during the winter of 1806-7 he gave four lectures — but his time was running out. He completed his fourth lecture — they had all been favourably received — and within a fortnight he was dead.

He was laid to rest in St Paul's alongside Sir Joshua Reynolds: Devon and Cornwall side by side as on the map.

One of his last paintings was of Doctor John Wolcot. There is a certain sadness in Wolcot's eyes. He almost certainly knew that time was running out, but, at least, he knew the boy from Cornwall had come a long way.

★ ★ ★ ★ ★

Following in the footsteps of another eccentric character, I veered back to Bodmin Moor. Near the Cheesewring Quarry I visited the remains of Daniel Gumb's hut, surely one of the oddest residences in the length and breadth of Cornwall, a fitting abode for a very odd

The remains of Gumb's hut: '. . . surely one of the oddest residences in the length and breadth of Cornwall.'

character. Daniel Gumb was a stonecutter from Linkinhorne — you can still see some of his work in the churchyard there.

Shortly after marrying, Gumb came to live in this wild, desolate spot in the first half of the eighteenth century. Richard Isbell, whose grandparents farmed on the Moor, had guided me up the slope from the village of Minions. As we stood at the mouth of the cave, we wondered how Mrs Gumb managed the catering in those pre-fridge, non deep-freeze days. Though we guessed she probably had bigger problems keeping the family warm and alive.

The quarry stands silent today, a reminder of past toil. But the Gumbs arrived before the quarry had begun or copper had been located close to the source of the Seaton. No village of Minions existed when the Gumbs came to settle here. Incredibly they raised a family in this bleak place. We tried to visualize the family home — and you need a constructive imagination because their rock shelter was demolished during quarrying and all that remains is a section of the capstone with a geometrical figure and some rain-water channelling, and rocks.

John Harris of Liskeard, visiting the cave a century and a half after the Gumbs had left, recalled: '. . . the entrance was rather low and narrow; the floor was full thirty feet long by ten or twelve feet wide, composed of sandy loam inclining towards one door, opposite which was a rude chimney. On the right hand side about three feet high was a bench of rock running nearly the whole length from three to four feet wide, along which ran a stout fir pole. This formed the sleeping place. On the left two other benches stood, one lower than the other, serving for sitting and table.'

These ruins apparently now lie roughly one hundred metres from the original site, and close to the edge of the quarry, where trainee mountain climbers practise today. Above, roughly half-way up the side of Stowe's Hill, is the Cheesewring.

Gumb interested himself in three subjects and the simple life: he studied mathematics, astronomy and philosophy. The loneliness here must have intensified Gumb's eccentricity. Yet we really know little of him. As far as I can ascertain, no hint of a picture of him exists. The meat of our knowledge of Daniel Gumb may cover more

◄ Visitors inspecting the Pythagoras
theorem carved by Daniel Gumb.

than the proverbial postage stamp, but literally not many postage stamps, for a letter to Richard Polwhele, written in September 1814, gives us a rare portrait in words of the man who turned his back on society:

'Daniel Gumb was born in the parish of Linkinhorne, in Cornwall, about the commencement of the last century, and was bred a stone-cutter. In the early part of his life he was remarkable for his love of reading and a degree of reserve even exceeding what is observable in persons of studious habits. By close application Daniel acquired, even in his youth, a considerable stock of mathematical knowledge, and, in consequence, became celebrated throughout the adjoining parishes. Called by his occupation to hew blocks of granite on the neighbouring commons, and especially in the vicinity of that great natural curiosity called the Cheesewring, he discovered near this spot an immense block, whose upper surface was an inclined plane. This, it struck him, might be made the roof of a habitation such as he desired; sufficiently secluded from the busy haunts of men to enable him to pursue his studies without interruption, whilst it was contiguous to the scene of his daily labour. Immediately Daniel went to work, and cautiously excavating the earth underneath, to nearly the extent of the stone above, he obtained a habitation which he thought sufficiently commodious. The sides he lined with stone, cemented with lime, whilst a chimney was made by perforating the earth at one side of the roof. From the elevated spot on which stood this extraordinary dwelling could be seen Dartmoor and Exmoor on the east, Hartland on the north, the sea and the port of Plymouth on the south, and St Austell and Bodmin hills on the west, with all the intermediate beautiful scenery. The top of the rock which roofed his house served Daniel for an observatory, where at every favourable opportunity he watched the motions of the heavenly bodies, and on the surface of which, with his chisel, he carved a variety of diagrams, illustrative of the most difficult problems of Euclid, etc. These he left behind him as evidence of the patience and ingenuity with which he surmounted the obstacles that his station in life had placed in the way of his mental improvement. But the choice of his house and the mode in which he pursued his studies were not his only eccentricities. His home became his chapel also; and he was never known to descend from the craggy mountain on which it stood, to attend his parish church or any other place of worship.

'Death, which alike seizes on the philosopher and the fool, at length found out the retreat of Daniel Gumb, and lodged him in a house more narrow than that which he had dug for himself.'

Anyway, when death did seize him, the clergyman at his funeral at Linkinhorne reflected: 'It is not for me to judge, suffice to say he has not been inside the church door for the last thirty years!'

If ever a man deserved a Moorland grave it was Daniel Gumb. However, at least, he has a splendid Moorland memorial. On the stone that formed part of the roof of his strange home is carved a geometrical diagram — the Pythagoras theorem — and his name and the date 1735 are carved on a neighbouring rock.

Visitors — quite a few no doubt — are puzzled by such marks. Daniel Gumb, I suspect, would have liked that. He puzzled many in his lifetime, and he remains a tantalizing figure in death. Maybe his ghost stalks this haunting, haunted landscape of the Moor.

The Night that Frightened Cornwall

Wednesday, 25 February 1981 was a night many people in parts of Cornwall will never forget. It was a night of alarm, fear, bewilderment — and earth tremors. The greatest chaos and anxiety was on the south western side of the county, around Falmouth and Penryn and the Lizard peninsula down to Penzance. The series of tremors were felt by some though as far north as Gunnislake; whereas residents in other areas heard nothing or assumed it was 'something to do with Concorde'.

Does Cornwall's geographical position perhaps make itself exposed or vulnerable to phenomena? William Borlase, in his *Natural History of Cornwall*, described how on the first day of November 1755 an earthquake killed as many as 300,000 Portuguese inhabitants, provoking the seas off the west coast of Cornwall to rise suddenly and dramatically by ten feet. Some students of the past believe this kind of phenomenon could have caused the flooding of Lyonesse. Of course, Lyonesse, like King Arthur, has grown into a bone of contention. Though now generally acknowledged as a legendary land, the medieval chroniclers did treat Lyonesse as an accepted geographical fact. There was also the 1090 tremor which allegedly destroyed part of St Michael's Mount.

Some may wonder about putting phenomena under a strange happenings umbrella. But there is no doubt about the reality of these tremors. One Falmouth resident told me, 'It was the worst night I've experienced since a really bad night in the Plymouth blitz!' I heard too of a dinner party at Penryn where cutlery bounced on the dining table and wine was spilt. Another resident, who claims to have seen a ghost, told me, 'I didn't mind seeing a ghost but I was bloody scared of those noises that February night!'

The first audible tremor took place around 7.15 — a rumble

lasting just three seconds followed by a bang that most people thought to be the nightly Concorde boom. Then came another tremor, just after half past eight, a repeat sequence but greatly intensified sending vibrations through buildings and spreading panic. From then until around midnight a series of minor booms took place at approximately twenty minute intervals.

The village of Constantine was the worst hit spot in the Falmouth-Penryn region, several properties suffering structural damage. Mrs A. Phelps of Rose Cottage, The Level, Constantine, told a *Falmouth Packet* reporter of 'cracks in her ceilings, with plaster falling to the floor in two of her rooms'. 'It sounded just like a bomb going off,' she said. Talking to *The Western Morning News,* Mrs Phelps expressed the view that the second bang was worst than the first. 'We had the plaster down from the ceiling on one side of the bedroom, and the chandelier just moved. We first thought it was an aeroplane crash in the valley below. The cottage moved. I've never seen anything like it. We have had the fire brigade people here looking around and the police are hopping around. They don't know what it is. It's shaken us all up completely. Our dogs went mad.'

The Western Morning News of 26 February gave the tremors front page treatment:

' "People were frightened and got in touch with us", a Falmouth Coastguard said. This was borne out by the fact that Penzance Police received about 300 telephone calls after the first disturbance which sounded like an explosion and that lines to Helston Police station were jammed.

'Eskdale Muir Observatory near Langholm, 600 km north of Cornwall, said that two tremors had registered on its seismic equipment.

'One woman told Penzance police that she was in the bath when the bang was heard . . . "I was out of the bath like a flash," she said.

'At Penzance, there was a report of a man's chair moving across the room with him sitting in it, and at Sennen a woman said she saw crockery jump up and down.

'At Helston, one of the tremors shook the council chamber while Kerrier District Council was in session.

'The major tremor at Helston brought people out into the streets.'

The Packet Group of Newspapers also gave the earth tremors considerable prominence. In addition to its interview with Mrs Phelps, *The Falmouth Packet* quoted another Constantine resident

Mrs Margaret Richards of 34 Wheal Vyvyan who said that cracks had appeared in the ceilings of three of her upstairs rooms following the tremors. 'I had only just painted the ceilings,' she said. 'There is a crack along the ceiling in my bedroom and plaster fell from the bathroom ceiling.'

Helston Packet reporters wrote of the following incidents: 'At Parc Eglos School, Helston, however, for pupils and staff arriving for school yesterday there was another shock. A floor in one classroom had moved considerably. The quarry tiles formed almost a pyramid shape and a crack ran the full length of the floor. Headmaster, Mr Geoff Helmore and teacher Mrs Di Devenish had little hesitation in re-organizing lessons for the day — and what better subject than earthquakes?

'Mr Brian Hodson, coastguard officer at Porthleven, admitted feeling the tremors and was then inundated with telephone calls from local residents.

'Lizard auxiliary coastguard Mr William Beringer, on duty at the lookout post at the time, said the whole building rattled. He too received numerous telephone calls from local residents and Cadgwith fisherman Mr Martin Ellis reported a large chair in his house being flung across the room.

'Mr Bill Kennedy, who lives at Cadgwith, said the tremor was particularly violent at about 8.30 p.m. Chairs and crockery moved in the houses and several items placed on shelves fell off.

'The tremors were probably the worst experienced in Cornwall for at least 150 years, according to the head of the seismology unit at the Institute of Geological Science in Edinburgh.

'Mr Chris Browitt told the *Falmouth Packet* that the worst tremors on Wednesday evening had been of intensity 5.'

The Cornishman of 5 March said 'many hundreds of telephone calls were answered by the police and coastguards around the area as local people wondered what had happened. The longest tremor lasted up to 15 seconds.

'Mr Tim Stevens, 25, an auxiliary coastguard, was in the bath at his home, lower Boscaswell, Pendeen. "I heard the rumbling like a heavy roller going past the house," he said later. "It lasted 12 to 15 seconds and was fairly loud. We are used to hearing Concorde, but this was more feeling than hearing. The house shook slightly and I could hear a couple of bottles on the shelf clinking together." '

Repercussions of the tremors were still being experienced a week later on the Lizard Peninsula. The Methodist Church at Mullion, for instance, had to close as a result of the shockwaves. The Reverend Leslie Goulden, the Methodist Minister, explained: 'A piece of plaster about ten feet square has moved, and it looks as though it could fall down. The builder said it's dangerous, and we have not used the church . . .'

Another to suffer was the Parish Church at Cury which has a two-stage tower. Here heavy corner stones in the tower had moved from their bedding. The Captain of the Bells, Henry Oates, felt the tower in too dangerous a condition for the bells to be rung. When it rains, water pours in through the cracks . . .'

Another interesting story dating from the night of the tremors came to me via Bossiney colleague Joy Francis. 'The beach at Millook,' she told me, 'has always been virtually a mass of big round pebbles, from egg size upwards. But on the morning after the

Looking out towards The Lizard: 'Does Cornwall's geographical position perhaps make itself exposed or vulnerable to such phenomena?'

tremors my brother went down on to the beach and it was changed dramatically . . . large pockets of sand where there had previously been just pebbles. It were as if some bulldozer had been driven along the beach and had swept them into small mountains. I was down on the beach recently with the family and the whole character of the beach has changed and it all dates from the night of the tremors.' The extraordinary thing about this account is that it happened high on the North Cornish coast, miles from the Lizard and Falmouth areas. One wonders just how many other bits of Cornwall were changed that night.

Among the older generation, more than one person said it all brought back memories of the War. 'It was like being in the middle of an air-raid,' as one put it. 'But the big difference was that in the war you had an air-raid warning and an all-clear, but on the night of 25 February we had neither . . . and all the time you were wondering, "What's going to happen next or is it all over?" ' Another man, who had been in the blitz, said: 'Then you knew the Germans were doing it, but that night in Cornwall you just didn't know who or what was causing this strange blitz.'

Among the people in West Cornwall to experience the two tremors on that Wednesday evening was Dr Keith Atkinson, a Principal Lecturer in Geology at the Camborne School of Mines. He was being interviewed over the telephone by a BBC radio reporter about his reactions to the first tremor when the second tremor occurred! 'The sensation was different from that caused by the nightly flights of Concorde,' said Dr Atkinson. 'It was less of an air blast and more of a ground vibration, causing loose objects on shelves in my home near Camborne to rattle.' The following day he was interviewed on BBC's radio programme 'Morning Sou'west' as well as on BBC and ITV television.

Comparing the tremors to earthquakes elsewhere Dr Atkinson explained that these major tremors probably would have been preceded by minor 'foreshocks' and would be followed by minor 'aftershocks' which might only be detected by the seismometers. On Thursday morning there was at least one aftershock strong enough to be felt. Asked to speculate on the likely cause of the tremors, Dr Atkinson suggested a slight movement on a geological fault, possibly in the Helston-Porthleven area.

Once the information from the network of seismographs had been unravelled the focus of the earthquake was identified as movement on a fault at a depth of four and a half kilometres below the hamlet of Nancenoy, about 1.5 kilometres due south of Constantine.

'So although Cornwall does not lie in one of the recognised major earthquake belts of the world,' Dr Atkinson told me, 'it has been suffering tremors of varying degrees of intensity certainly since the eleventh century and probably much earlier. The reasons for these earthquakes are many but probably most are related to the numerous geological faults, of many ages and differing sizes, which criss-cross the county. Slight movement on one of these faults, relieving pent-up stresses in the earth's crust, caused the tremors of that Wednesday and Thursday in February 1981.'

Arthur Reincarnated

Enthusiasm for Arthur is no recent development. Elizabeth Jenkins in her excellent *The Mystery of King Arthur,* recalled two examples from the long-ago.

In 1220, an abbot was addressing the monks in his chapter house: 'Seeing that many, especially of the lay brethren, were asleep, and that some were even snoring, he cried out: "Hark, brethren, Hark! I will tell you of something new and great. There was once a mighty King, whose name was Arthur!" The effect was electric. The abbot then said: "Had they not come to a sad pass, when they would not stay awake to hear of holy things, but were agog at the mention of Arthur?"

'This far-flung fame would scarcely have been achieved in a later world where there were more stories to compete, but even so it was extraordinary. The story was not only spell-binding: it aroused deep, passionate conviction. In 1146, Herman de Tournai related that some of the canons of Laon Cathedral were in Cornwall on a fund-raising mission. They arrived at Bodmin carrying an image of Our Lady which they declared had power to heal. A man with a withered arm presented himself, but before the healing influence could be invoked, an unseemly fracas had broken out. "Just as the Bretons were wont to wrangle with the French on behalf of King Arthur, the man began to dispute with one of our company, saying Arthur was still living." So great was the feeling aroused, "it came to bloodshed", and the cure could not be performed.'

Was there a King Arthur? And if he did exist, was he really linked to the Westcountry?

Those two questions have baffled and fascinated many. But one man thinks he has some of the answers to the Arthurian puzzle — through mind travel. Barney Camfield of Plymouth, a Natural Healing Therapist and Unitarian Minister, feels Arthur belonged to

Barney Camfield of Plymouth believes Arthur belonged
to reality. 'Arthur had a pretty strong "alpha" wave, the
kind you would find . . . in those who *know* they will be successful.'

reality: a truly historical figure in the same factual mould as say Sir Francis Drake or Raleigh. Arthur, in his opinion, is no vague legendary character — who may or may not have been.

'Arthur, I would say, was a bit of a hellion. He suffered, he tells me, from prostate trouble later in life. Quite a womanizer he admits, but later he matured and became more spiritual. Arthur had a pretty strong "alpha" wave, the kind you would find in successful sprinters, businessmen and those who *know* without doubt that they will be successful. Healers have the same wave which shows up on an E.C.G. I demonstrated it on a Westward TV programme a few years ago. Arthur was like an Eton man; it was instilled in him — he was conditioned — to be a Ruler or leader.

'Melanus, or Merlin, acted as a Kissinger type and got the tribes together in 474 AD at what is now Camel's Head on the Tamar. The nearest settlement was on St Michael's Island but the local tribal leader wouldn't allow a meeting on the island. Observers, when viewing the island . . . Drake's Island . . . at that time say it was much larger. Actually the water level was lower, and there was a causeway joining it to Cornwall.

'Breton and other tribal leaders met there, as Arthur states, but I would say that it wasn't exactly an election . . . the others were persuaded to elect him! Arthur had the charisma and the ability to get others to do what he wanted. He didn't do much persuading himself . . . felt he didn't need to . . . because the others needed him to be in overall command and get the Saxons on the run.

'Arthur did a sort of tour of Cornwall, a recruiting tour perhaps, and did go back occasionally. The sword given to him at Tintagel was from Ireland. Merlin, in a previous incarnation as an Irish chieftain, was also a herbalist, healer and smith . . . he made it.'

Barney Camfield reckons he knows Merlin well too. Moreover he makes a remarkable claim, relating Merlin to Cornwall.

'Merlin or Melanus or Mellion, was a Druidic-Mithraic-Christian Bishop. In other words, whilst ostensibly Christian the other religions had greatly influenced him and he knew quite a bit about herbalism and healing and other like matters, Psycho-expansion for instance. You'll find Merlin mentioned in the parish church at St

◀ Merlin's Cave at Tintagel: 'Merlin acted as a
Kissinger type and got the tribes together . . .'

Mellion in connection with battles in Brittany. There's a plaque on the wall in the church there. Most people don't equate this St Mellion with Merlin or Melanus . . . but he was the same.'

Barney Camfield makes these astonishing revelations, not basically on the strength of historical research or reading but on a personal psychic experience. He says, 'I was around in Arthurian times and I have made this contact with Arthur and people close to him through our psycho-expansion groups.'

The principal uses of psycho-expansion are to allow individuals to know themselves more deeply and to recognize and understand how different other people's habits and personalities can be, particularly when the individual is returned to his or her former life or lives. The basic understanding is that we keep returning to this Earthly life until we finally work out our salvation.

Outside and beyond all this, Barney Camfield aids people in their present lives, using the same methods as a form of psychotherapy.

On the group's ability to recapture — or relive the past — Barney Camfield admits they make no claims as to *how* they are able to get such accurate observations through relaxation. Sometimes, he says, dates or details may get distorted.

'Others involved in this kind of work report, as does Arthur Guirdham, that groups are tending together apparently accidently. This seems to have happened with quite a number of people here. If I made any suggestion as to what would be "seen" this would more than likely be accepted and produced. I simply say, "Go back to 450 AD" or whatever. Then after a period of time — five, ten, fifteen minutes — I suggest they open their eyes and write down their recollections. They are also aware of being "here" in time and space as well as travelling to and from in time and space.'

The crystals are important in the Arthurian story because they were used in connection with communication and power. On the subject of the crystals, Barney Camfield says: 'They're interesting. They were often in gold containers because they gave out radiation and gold shielded one from the radiation. We have tracked these crystals from Atlantis to Egypt to Moses. They were used in the

◄St Mellion Church: 'There's a plaque on the wall . . .
Most people don't equate this St Mellion with Merlin
or Melanus . . . but he was the same.'

Ark, which was why Moses and Aaron had to wear protective clothing . . . see relevant portions of the Bible. Later the crystals were used and kept by the Essenes and had Yeshua (Jesus) been successful in taking over as Priest King in Judea they would have been fitted back into the Ark. Later Merlin used a crystal or crystals.'

By a fascinating coincidence, just before learning about Barney Camfield's psycho-expansion group and their Arthurian connection, author Colin Wilson, gave me a copy of his book *Strange Powers*. In it Colin wrote about three people possessing such powers.

It was the third character who really attracted my attention: Dr Arthur Guirdham, a respected British physician, who is convinced he is a reincarnated member of a thirteenth century religious sect, about which he has written in considerable detail — and with mysterious accuracy.

There will, of course, be plenty of cynics on the idea of a group of thirteenth century Cathars being resurrected in twentieth century Britain. Likewise there will be 'Doubting Thomases' protesting about Barney Camfield's reincarnated 'Arthurian set'.

The interesting thing that the three people in Colin Wilson's book — the others being a retired sales manager in Sussex, Robert Leftwich, who is not only a dowser but who has made journeys out of his physical body, and Eunice Beattie, a nurse who has written hundreds of pages of predictions, dictated by spirits — all consider their powers normal. If that's correct, then are the rest of us abnormal? Or are we somehow subnormal?

As Colin Wilson perceptively concludes: '. . . the day when Occultists and Spiritualists had to plead to be taken seriously is past. Certain facts are lying around where scientists cannot help tripping over them. And that is a situation which the tidy mind of the scientist finds intolerable. As Charles Fort might have expressed it: If the Occult did not exist, science would be compelled to invent it.'

The following notes have been compiled by Barney Camfield on the evidence of members of the group going back to Arthurian times. In view of the sensational claims that these people were, in fact, once famous figures belonging to a distant past, they are not willing to reveal their identities.

The reincarnationist will find much of it fascinating and feasible, but those who do not accept reincarnation will dismiss it entirely.

ARTHUR

Born around 450-455 AD in South Wiltshire. Earliest recollection as a little boy playing in the courtyard of a Roman villa. Mother: small with long fair hair, wearing a long purple dress, plain gold circlet around her head.

Father: not sure, but a tremendous bond with a man who 'feels' like my father: broad-shouldered, short, dark curly hair, round dark eyes. Medium height. Taught me all 'manly' pursuits when a boy. Gave me a knife — like a dagger — used it as a sword when small. Took me up in front of him on horse.

Bishop Melanus visited here briefly when I was little. Talked with Ambrosius, my 'father'. He is always dressed as a Roman soldier. Around the age of fifteen, went to Brittany — seemed like a gathering of Celtic 'clans'.

About 475 in a small boat moving up the River Tamar. Camp-like conditions: trees in leaf, fire in clearing, making of weapons.

In a small boat with others moving towards St Michael's Island. Melanus met me dressed as a monk: black-dark habit. Walked with him talking, along a path made of large blocks, granite, neatly set. Chapel. Knelt in front of Melanus who placed hands on my head: blessing. Meeting of other tribal leaders in long hut. Look a very rough mob . . . smell awful!

Artos, the Bear, physically very strong, powerful. As a young man feels ruthless, able to control, gets what he wants. Not gentle in any way. Womaniser. Acts and reacts to situations as with animal instincts. Acute sense of smell, hearing and sight. Absolute target with axe throw. Has part Roman (leather) clothing. At one time wearing lamb's skin over shoulders. When in battle legs bound up with wide strips soft leather. Had helmet in early days fitting crown of head. Later on seemed to have pieces attached rather like Viking helmets. Breast plate for earlier battles, changed in the last two or three to one with an equilateral cross. Last big battle — Badon — a red stone set in centre of cross. Also cross on back plate. Latterly rode a white horse — much better specimen than earlier ones which were very small like moorland ponies — long shaggy hair. In contrast, others were like carthorses.

Moved from meeting of tribal leaders with small company of men down into Cornwall — so many trees everywhere! — to monastery type place on cliffs. North Cornwall — think it was Tintagel. Went down steps below chapel — a sort of crypt with niches in walls — a burial chamber. A sword in silver scabbard with runic markings on it, and handle area jewelled, was given to me. It had come from Ireland some time ago. A Saint connected — Patrick I think.

Ambrosius had died around 474 AD.

St Michael's Island meeting: 476-8.

On the Tamar: 'About 475 in a small boat moving up the Tamar. Camp-like conditions: trees in leaf, fire in clearing, making of weapons.'

**'Moved from meeting of tribal leaders . . .
down to Cornwall . . . to monastery type place
on cliffs. North Cornwall — think it was Tintagel.'**

Thence to Cornwall. Gathered men on way back to Somerset. On to a battle in the Midlands. Across to North Wales: Battle. Artos receiving clairaudience through fighting. Over to North East England: Battle. During this time Arthur met Merlin — Melanus — in a forest on borders with Wales: a building of stone. Inside wall with painted symbols. Here Merlin showed Arthur a large leather-bound book full of symbols.

Sister bending over me, and others. Move down towards bottom of hill where some buildings of wood. One of stone, long and low. Has centre courtyard — Monastery. Waiting for Melanus. He comes. Have discussion and move into chapel together. By this time Arthur has become a more thoughtful person. Intuition had been enhanced. Could clearly 'see' extra-terrestrial beings. This last exercise at Glastonbury *lent* him — me — the strength required for

57

last years. Last great battle significant — Mt Badon. About 505 AD Wiltshire I think. Mordred — son — one of my Commanders, looks very like me: fair hair, eyes and shape of face the same, but slighter in proportions all round. He hates me, I can see it in his eyes: jealous.

Final battle location unknown. Am being carried through forest of beautiful trees. My legs badly damaged and in great pain. Seemed to eventually arrive at Glastonbury Monastery. Very ill. Sister Morgan — Morwenna — with me and giving healing. Died 518 AD.

Another small 'cameo'. Standing on high cliffs, looked like North Devon or Wales and looking out from derelict stone-built circular look-out for boats coming from Ireland. Joined by Percival (cousin) who gave something into my hand — not sure what — a key or a stone?

Meeting of five tribal leaders of Britain inside brightly coloured room. Metal table on which stood five pewter-looking jars (classical shape — fluted edges). Discussion on coming battle and placing of tribes. Lots cast with a feather to decide.

GERAINT

Merlin — a title given to a 'Druidic Monk' who practised the best of the Old Religion and Celtic Christianity. Melanus or Mellion was one who was known as Merlin and he spent some time on St Michael's Island — Drake's Island — where he received sons of Tribal Lords of Devon and Cornwall to be initiated into the Ancient Knowledge.

These young men were to become the leaders who gathered together (probably at Camel's Head — the nearest suitable meeting point to the Island), and elected Arturus to be the one to head them against the Saxon invaders. Another of these was Geraint, Prince of

**Arthur being offered 'Excalibur'
by the Lady of the Lake — painting by Hatherell. ▶**

Dumnonia, who was greatly influenced by his training with Merlin on the Island. He felt he was destined for more than warfare. When — after several battles — Geraint was injured and unable to ride or fight, he sought out Merlin again and learnt more of the Ancient Arts. He became aware that there were in England several ancient artifacts containing crystals of power whose use was long forgotten. He set out to seek for these and eventually arrived at Glastonbury. By other means Arturus and others also came here and the crystals came to light. They were taken from earth and not to be used until they could be returned and put to proper use by those who had the knowledge.

MORGANA

Born 478 AD Roman type villa near Old Sarum, about one and a half miles away from the present day Salisbury in Wiltshire. Dressed in Roman style and lived in a Roman type villa.

Half sister to Arthur — same Mother. Met Merlin when I was about eight years old. He came to the villa looking for me. Later took me away and taught me all the things I would need to know. I had a stone circle that I used a lot just to the north of the villa.

Later used Glastonbury Tor. Temple built there, with stone circle around it. Inside magnificent mosaic floor, set out with twelve pointed star, each point lining up with the stone column outside. The twelve signs of the zodiac were set between each point of the star. This Temple was used to give Arthur a spiritual boost when needed. I had six other helpers. At one time we sat cross-legged on the floor and tried to hold back the enemy with thought power.

After Arthur's last battle which was some sort of civil war he was killed and I fled to Glastonbury with the crystal in the gold bowl. Percival was with me. We hid the crystal in the rock which we could open and close with thought power. Then we fled into Wales where I died in 512 AD.

The most sensational event of this whole exploration into the Arthurian story was one sunlit April afternoon, when I met a member of Barney Camfield's group. A Westcountry housewife, with brown eyes, she claims to have been Arthur in an earlier life. In addition to being a wife and a mother, she does healing work and has her own psycho-expansion group. Bearing in mind what happened in Bodmin all those years ago, when someone claimed that Arthur was still alive, I could understand her wish to remain anonymous!

She began regression in July 1979. I asked how regression works. 'We relax into a state of heightened consciousness, the Alpha state. Briefly, the brain, as Colin Wilson has explained, has two halves: the left is the analytical side, while the right observes patterns and colours and is intuitive. The tendency is to rely too much on the left in modern life. Generally, I believe, man is not realizing his full potential. Through this shift in the level of consciousness you become more aware, more perceptive rather like tuning into your own "mind computer".

'The discovery of my apparent life as Arthur, Artos, which is a very honest and real, albeit at times quite shattering, experience to me, is only one of my many other apparent lives . . . some very ordinary and others extraordinary.

'I make no claims — I'm only willing to share a small portion, at the moment, of a happening which may help or be useful to others who are willing to search. I'm willing to say, however, that Arthur lives, and that the idea which this name engenders is only part of a mystery involving us all and, once begun, I feel the quest must continue.

'The evidence I've gathered during my work in psycho-expansion, in the past two years, fills over a dozen notebooks. This evidence is written down from my experiences. I do not expect anyone to believe my evidence — why should I? However, I do hope that the reader will keep his or her mind open in order to recognize possibilities, when more and more people all over the world are discovering and reporting about their journeys and experiments with the mind.

'If you are a seeker, then your experiences will begin to make sense the more you search. I often say after travelling in time and space: "I wish I could bring you back something from the places and times where I have been." Even if this happened, there would still be those who would keep their minds closed — perhaps this is because everyone is at a different stage of awareness in their own

**Arthur's appearance: '. . . many writers
have got him wrong.'**

personal life's journey.

'My observation to the reader is: accept and believe nothing you are told as being conclusive evidence. Why? Because once you draw a conclusion, you cease to look for further evidence, and if this should nevertheless be presented, then you have a conflict, sometimes deep within you. Every day, new discoveries are made, and so it is with the mind.'

'Isn't it strange that now you're a woman and then you were a man?'

'No,' she explained, 'some people come back to this life many times, and in very different forms . . . there seem to be no rules, save those of cause and effect.'

I then asked when she went back to Arthur's time was it as Arthur in action or merely as an observer?

She looked thoughtful: 'It's rather like going to a cinema or theatre and joining in the action, and it's not just an isolated thing. I've been back something like twelve to fifteen times, usually for about five to ten minutes.

'I've never been a serious historian though always interested in stones and stone circles. At first, I didn't know I was Arthur. It was only when someone asked me my name that it came out.'

'Wasn't that shattering?'

She laughed. 'Absolutely shattering! Am I going mad, I wondered?'

But her face suddenly went serious. 'I'm not deluded. I know what I know. When I go back to that earlier life, I feel genuine emotions: love, fear, hatred and so on . . . I'm inside Arthur. Now I have brown eyes. Then I had blue. I feel very Roman . . . more Roman than many of the scholars and historians think, and though I wasn't born this time in Cornwall — I was born in Devon — I feel a great affinity with things Celtic. On camping holidays down in Penwith, sleeping under canvas, close to the ground, I feel very at home.

'Getting back to Arthur's appearance, many writers have got him wrong. But when I heard a description of the novelist Rosemary Sutcliffe's on a BBC radio programme, I tingled with excitement because it was me . . . it was Arthur . . . and I must stress that I only heard the radio programme *after* I had begun with the psycho-expansion group and had gone back to Arthur's time.'

Big-boned as a Jute and brown skinned, under hair the colour of a hayfield when it pales at harvest time, Huh, I suppose that I must have had all that from my mother, for assuredly there was nothing there of dark narrow-boned Ambrosius' nor consequently of Uther, his brother and my father, who men had told me was like him. On campaign I generally grew my beard and clipped it short, but in winter quarters I always tried to keep a smooth chin in the Roman manner.

'Rosemary Sutcliffe imagined Arthur in that way in her book *Sword at Sunset,* and when I heard those words on radio, I was amazed.

'Today I'm an Aquarian,' she explained, 'but then as Arthur I was Aries. That fits, of course, Aries, the first sign of the Zodiac, a natural for leadership.' She gesticulated with her hands, emphasising the now and the then. Her current Aquarian status fits too, in the sense that characteristic of this, the eleventh sign of the

Zodiac, she is very involved in causes and service: a healer, a committed conservationist, and concerned in the welfare and future of society.

'Arthur had this great charisma. But he wasn't the chivalrous character that some of the story-tellers would have us believe. As a young man he was keen on women and fathered as many as fifteen children in various parts of Britain by various women.'

Lyonesse has always fascinated me, that lost land which has fired the imagination of generations of men and women. It has been said that Lyonesse was above water in Arthur's reign and that it lies sunken between Land's End and Scilly. Some have claimed the Scillies as the high peaks of Lyonesse. So inevitably our conversation turned to that landscape which has featured in so many Arthurian versions. 'Yes' she said, 'there were definitely some extra areas of land visible off the coast of Land's End Peninsula, particularly off the most southerly points. As I can also "see" forward I can tell you that it will reappear, and I see Atlantis reappearing too.'

The most fascinating part of our interview came near the end when the interviewee offered to go back in time for me. 'Where would you like me to go?' she asked.

Remembering those notes and the reference to receiving a sword at Tintagel, I had no doubts.

Within moments rather than minutes, she appeared to be in a trance, her voice noticeably lower in key, and assuming an intensity that was not there earlier, she described travelling with a group of men and pack horses through a wooded valley and coming to the coast, to a building there.

Either my hostess was a very convincing actress or I was watching and listening to an extraordinary event. Her voice changed: at times she was worried, 'trouble coming from the north', at other moments she was amused, 'I can *smell* the herbs from the beautifully sheltered gardens'. Then there was an excitement in her voice: 'Oh, I've now discovered the purpose of this place and this group; it's a kind of hospital, and these are the ones who came over from Brittany.' It was no matter-of-fact commentary, no plateau of emotion or response to the events. 'You never see many people about here' were words expressed on journeying through the wooded valley; here I heard the voice of an experienced traveller, someone who had been this way on previous occasions. Her experience of receiving the sword — not Excalibur — from the hands of an unknown hooded figure had an awe about it: an element of something religious or royal, rather as you might speak in a Cathedral.

There was a sense of geography too. 'There's activity along this coast, a definite link with Ireland, but there's more movement down the coast . . . there's a trade route there,' an obvious reference to the Camel.

She came out of her state gradually, almost like someone awakening from a deep sleep or dream. In my bones I felt she had journeyed a long way; there was more than a hint of a weary traveller arriving at a destination, or getting back.

Barney Camfield refers to this condition as 'relaxation of the mind . . . then comes what was termed by Goethe "contemplative perception". I don't know of a better way to describe it.'

**'Remembering those notes and the reference
to receiving a sword at Tintagel . . .'**

On the Camel: '. . . there's a trade route there.'

Reflecting on this particular journey back, she said: 'The fact I found so interesting was that there seemed to be such a lot of travelling going on between Brittany and Cornwall, Devon and Dorset, and also the strong link with Ireland.

'When I, Artos, was looking out from the derelict stone-built tower on the north coast, I was pacing up and down scanning the horizon for the sails of the boats from Ireland, with a feeling of great anxiety and expectancy. I know I needed their help, and was excited at the prospect of meeting with a friend or friends again.

'You can imagine how difficult and frustrating it is to only tune in for short periods and bring back snatches of what one person was experiencing at that time. The fact that he was so in tune with Nature and so observant and keen with his senses is a terrific help since there must be a great deal more stored in the memory bank. If, for instance, I, Artos, had lost the sight of my eyes in the last battle, or indeed if you are blind in any previous lives, the curtain comes down so to speak, and one is left with the emotion and physical experiences largely. I can certainly say that I cannot face the times of the actual battles and fighting and go through them. The intensity and the visual experiences are so horrific as to make the blood run cold so to speak. Having glimpsed some of it I can "pull out" and leave well alone.

'There is no doubt in my mind that in time, this work will become more common-place, and we will be accepted as metal detectors are used now. Mental detectors! Historians and scholars and physicists all might be helped with their theories. Some won't like it either!

'Barney and members of the group have a great deal of courage to allow themselves to be accused as deluded mental cases, as undoubtedly we will be labelled by some. It is the very fact that I feel this work, which is so valuable for healing, must be improved, recognised and put to good use, that I am willing to help with these experiences.'

Back in St Teath, I told a Bossiney colleague of the interview. 'Did you really believe you had interviewed King Arthur?' she asked.

I found it a difficult question to answer. 'I'm convinced the lady in question is convinced she was Arthur.' That was my reply on the spot. That is my considered opinion now.

Beyond the Grave?

Alan Nance is not a strange character. He is a remarkable man.

He and his team of helpers at 24 Trevarthian Road, St Austell, have been the agents of some great healing work. But he makes no special claims, knowing, he says, 'that we're merely the channels of a healing process.'

I have an idea that Alan Nance may be amused to find Spiritualism inside the covers of a book on Strange Happenings. The fact is he talks of spirit people in the way most of us talk about friends or relations, our neighbours or business associates. The spirit people — to Alan Nance — are no vague, mystical figures. He sees them as intensely alive and capable of communion with us in this Earthly life. 'We are the clods!'

Anyone, who is not a Spiritualist, could find conversation with him a slightly disconcerting experience, but there is no hint of 'talking down' or preaching in any discussion with this incredibly 'young' blue-eyed Scillonian. Indeed you soon get the idea that he is not impressed by the posturing of some religious leaders — he's firmly convinced the message is more important than any messenger.

Moreover, he has no doubts about Life beyond the grave or the crematorium — and this was why I was interviewing him at his home.

At the age of eighty-three, he has no fear of the thing we call death.

'Death's only a door opening,' he explained. 'I have no fear of it whatsoever. When the time comes for me to go, I shall go without regrets. Death, when it comes, will come as a friend. This material world is the fantasy. The other, their world, is the reality. Recently when I had a bad bout of flu, I thought it's time to go. But my guide told me firmly there's still work to be done on this side. So I didn't argue . . . but I could have gone happily.

'I have seen people, who have passed on, very vividly. Most people would say they'd seen a ghost, but I'd prefer to say that such appearances are proof of the Hereafter. I saw my first ghost when I was in my teens. I had gone to bed and in the street outside the bedroom there was this bright street light shining . . . I saw a woman in black . . . in this light she looked a perfectly normal woman . . . and then she slowly disappeared.

'Here's another example. Just a few years ago, I was down in Breage in West Cornwall, visiting the sister of an old friend . . . I say old friend though Carrie passed over when she was only thirty-six. I used to go down there to see her sister Elizabeth. One afternoon I was sitting there, and I dozed off and as I awoke there was Carrie, the Carrie I knew. No, it wasn't a question of dreaming and seeing her in a dream. She was standing there in front of me very clearly. My guide made contact with me and told me how pleased Carrie was that I had seen her.

'Had she changed? Grown older?' I asked.

'No, in every instance, she was the young woman I knew. I think when those, who have passed on, appear to us on this side, they reappear as they were for identification purposes. It's a kind of confirmation if you like. There is no old age in the spirit world, it is only the body which deteriorates, the spirit is ageless. Do you remember the line in the 11 November ceremonies: "They shall not grow old as we who are left grow old." Whoever wrote that line knew the truth.'

A hearing aid is one of Alan Nance's few concessions to advancing years. A stranger would place him years younger. He continues to lead a very full life, holding healing sessions two days a week, and happily doing more in cases of emergency. 'No, it doesn't tire me,' he said, 'in fact, after a long healing session I often feel stronger.' His handshake is firm, but his words come softly. His grasp of the subject in conversation is remarkable and his vocabulary extraordinary when you learn his schooldays ended at the age of thirteen, while the books, lining his bookcase, clearly reflect his great interests: Spiritualism and healing, and his love of Cornwall and Scilly where he was born.

Our conversation turned inevitably to his guide.

'My spirit guide is a North American Indian. He lived on Earth more than seven hundred years ago . . . I know his name but I've never seen him. But other people have described him to me . . . mediums have seen him . . . I get the messages from him. Just before going to sleep for the night or first thing in the morning are the best times. Then you're more relaxed, more responsive.

'Christine, one of my healers, saw him recently, and some time ago when I was staying in a boarding house, the landlady there knew I was a Spiritualist through various literature lying about in my room. "There's another Spiritualist living downstairs," she said. So I went down to see this person, and when she opened the door to let me in she remarked: "Oh, I see you've got an Indian with you." She could see my guide as clearly as she could see me.

'I've also been told that Silver Birch helps me quite a bit as a spirit guide. He has been for years guide of Hannen Swaffer's home circle in London, and his spirit teachings have been put into book form by Spiritualists.'

Silver Birch has clearly been a big influence on Alan Nance's life and growth as a Spiritualist. 'Our allegiance is not to a Creed, not to a Book, not to a Church, but to the Great Spirit of Life and His eternal natural laws.' That briefly is Silver Birch's philosophy, and Alan Nance has those words framed in his healing room at St Austell. Trevarthian Road slopes high above the local station and that railway line which stretches from Penzance to Paddington.

On the subject of our state after death, Alan Nance referred me to some thoughts conveyed by Silver Birch through a medium. In answer to a question about whether we retain our earth names, Silver Birch explained: 'Yes, as long as it is necessary for a person to be so identified. But what you must remember is that the name is not the individual; it is only the means by which he is known — once you have passed beyond the magnetic field of the earth, the name does not matter because you are then known for the individual that you truly are . . . once you have got beyond the earthly pull, once you have passed the stage of earthly association and reached the span to which you are thus entitled, you emit a light, an aura, a radiation, which indicates who and what you are.'

Alan Nance is not a medium: 'I haven't quite the confidence, but I

Spiritualist and healer Alan Nance: 'Those who have passed on from the beginning of time are still around us . . . time and space have no meaning in the spirit world.' ▶

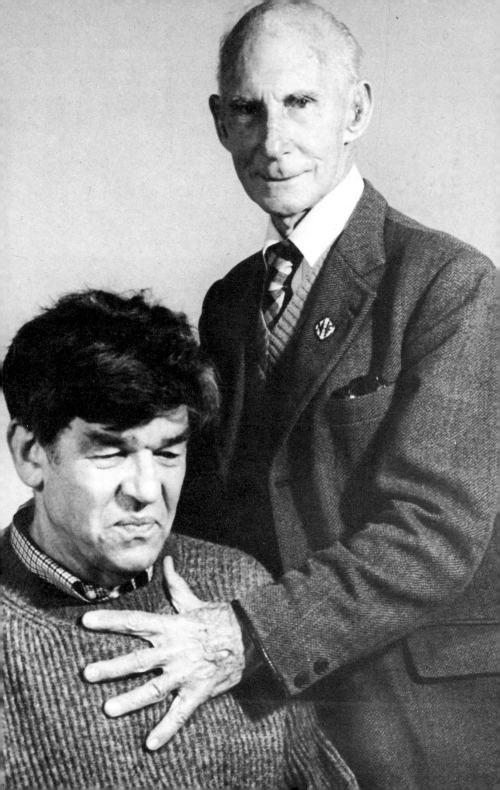

once acted as a medium. A woman contacted me in a terrible state. Her son-in-law had gone off and she was terribly worried. "Will he come back? Or shall we never see him again?" I said I'd do my best; came back home and here my guide told me the young man would be back very soon. So I promptly phoned her up and said don't worry . . . he'll soon be back. It was four o'clock in the afternoon, and by six o'clock the son was home!'

'Do you actually hear your guide speak?' I asked.

'Some Spiritualists hear an audible voice, but I don't. Things are imprinted on my mind . . . words form themselves very quickly and very clearly. We should not underestimate the spirit world . . . it's highly intelligent, able to communicate clearly and at great speed.'

'Mediums, though, have had rather a bad press haven't they? Some have been exposed as bogus.'

'That's true and, of course, it's a field that leaves itself wide open to exploitation by the phoney. But there are bogus bank managers, bogus doctors. You'll find phoney people in every walk of life. It's the bogus medium that makes the news, not the good one.'

Alan Nance believes the evidence of life after death is overwhelming. 'Thousands and thousands of messages have been received from the other side — all the people can't be under some grand delusion. On one occasion in London, with two friends, I suggested we should visit the Spiritualist Association of Great Britain in Belgrave Square. It was a group sitting with about twenty people present. The medium is there for an hour picking out people to whom she wishes to pass on information she is receiving concerning them. Her first statement to me was, "You have a brother and a sister in the spirit world." I replied, "Yes." And the medium went on to say "It's your brother I wish to speak to you about: the greatest surprise he ever had was to find he was still alive when he passed over."

'The important thing here was that my brother was an atheist. All his life he firmly disbelieved in *any* life after death.

'Then there was an interesting point about my father's death. He had a great love of toast, and after he'd passed over, the whole house was permeated with the smell of toast. That smell of toast even followed me to Australia . . . so you see distance doesn't deter the spirit world.

'The spirit world's capable of tremendous leg-pulls . . . Apporting — that's the capacity of spirit to transport material objects without

72

material aids — I've had many experiences of this. Once I lost my bunch of keys. I was so convinced they'd gone that I had my lock changed and then they reappeared . . . no, it wasn't a coincidence or a question of mislaying them. It was one of many instances where things have been apported.

'Edna, one of my healers, always removed all her rings before she began a healing session. One day they all vanished but they were returned.'

Alan Nance talks with a sincerity that would dent most cynicism. You find yourself asking 'Why would a man of his integrity want to invent something like this?'

Just before our interview at St Austell, Alan Nance had sent me an extract from *Man and the Spiritual World* by the Reverend Arthur Chambers, something published at the turn of the century. Taking the form of a reported seance, it tells the story of a not particularly well-educated young Englishman acting as the medium, and how under trance he was capable of speaking fluently in Hindustani.

'Isn't that stretching our credibility a bit too far?' I probed.

Alan Nance laughed: 'Not a bit of it. I heard a French medium, in a trance state, speak cut-glass English which she never used in her normal Australian conversation! She was a French woman living down under.'

'Isn't it going to be a bit crowded on the other side, when you think of all the people who have lived since the beginning of time?'

Alan Nance laughed again. 'Come off it, Michael, you're more intelligent than that! Our vision is very limited . . . you love those cliffs at Tintagel . . . well, the view there stretches out to sea for miles and miles but what you're seeing is only a drop in the ocean. If this world can be on such a scale, we can't begin to imagine the scale on the other side.

'Life on this side and the other is all involved in vibration. When we pass over, our vibration is commensurate with the life we have lived on earth. This is our passport . . . no Judgement Day . . . we are our own judges. We go to a position in keeping with this vibration, *nothing can alter that,* be it good, bad or indifferent. Spiritual progress is possible on the other side; as the vibration increases these people then become invisible to those who have just passed over. "Heaven" is not "up there", that is an extended physical world. Those who have passed on from the beginning of time are still around us . . . time and space have no meaning in the spirit world.

'Where I disagree with the great majority of Church people is that I don't accept the Divinity of Christ, that He was God in human form . . . I don't go along with the idea that God's an Englishman with a long white beard sitting on a throne!'

But Alan Nance doesn't let his Spiritualism necessarily parade in his work as a Spiritual healer. 'I'm happy to heal people of all faiths or none and they don't need to believe in me! There have been cases where a patient has been dragged along for healing by a relation or friend in desperation . . . and it still works. I'm only sorry doctors don't send more people to healers. Healing, for instance, can work wonders with asthma.

As our conversation came to an end we returned to the theme of life on earth today.

'Life's a school,' Alan Nance said as he finished his Earl Grey tea, 'a preparation for life on the other side. It's a natural law. Yes, it is a kind of examination . . . and we mark the papers . . . through our vibrations we know where to go. People on the other side don't all go on the same level. The Bible's right: "In my Father's house are many mansions." There'll be no Judgement Day, no Judge and Jury. You'll be your own Judge.

'We are all God's children, regardless of colour, race or creed or no creed. It is *how* we live that matters.'

Meeting Alan Nance, that April afternoon, was a tonic. In a week when murder, warfare in Northern Ireland, cheque book journalism, political infighting and intrigue made the headlines in our newspapers, when radio and television expressed shoals of bad news with scarcely a hint of anything good, Alan Nance's positive approach to life and death was wonderfully refreshing.

As I drove back through the china-clay country everything took on a brighter, almost summery glow — it was as if the calendar had suddenly inexplicably advanced. I reflected that maybe time isn't quite as important as we sometimes make it. Or perhaps I was just looking at the landscape — and life — in a different light.

Three Holy Wells

From Alan Nance to a tour among some of Cornwall's ancient wells is a natural logical step. The link, of course, is healing.

Robert Hunt, on his journeys across Cornwall more than half a century ago paid special attention to our Cornish wells. 'A spring of water has always something about it which gives rise to holy feelings,' he said. 'From the dark earth there wells up a pellucid fluid, which in its apparent tranquil joyousness gives gladness to all around. The velvet mosses, the swordlike grasses, and the feathery ferns, grow with more of that light and vigorous nature which indicates a fullness of life, within the charmed influence of a spring of water, than they do elsewhere.

'The purity of the fluid impresses itself, through the eye, upon the mind, and its power of removing all impurity is felt to the soul. "Wash and be clean," is the murmuring call of the waters, as they overflow their rocky basins, or grassy vases; and deeply sunk in depravity must that man be who could put to unholy uses one of nature's fountains. The inner life of a well of waters, bursting from its grave in the earth, may be religiously said to form a type of the soul purified by death, rising into a glorified existence and the fullness of light. The tranquil beauty of the rising waters, whispering the softest music, like the healthful breathing of a sleeping infant, sends a feeling of happiness through the soul of the thoughtful observer, and the inner man is purified by its influence, as the outer man is cleansed by ablution.

'Water cannot be regarded as having an inanimate existence. Its all-pervading character and its active nature, flowing on for ever, resting never, removes it from the torpid elements, and places it, like the air, amongst those higher creations which belong to the vital powers of the earth . . .'

Cornwall's magical atmosphere defies a simple single explanation. The ingredients are almost certainly a mixture of material and mystical, and owing little or nothing to man. Yet I've always thought our Cornish wells have been an important factor. Many of them have an aura.

It was as a small boy that I visited my first well: Madron Well, high above Penzance. Though that small boy didn't understand the full significance on that first exploration, the impression of something holy, like a church or chapel, stuck in the memory. Moreover that boyhood impression came flooding back recently when I was researching at the Local Studies Department of the Cornwall County Library at Redruth.

Bottrell, in his *Traditions of West Cornwall* said: 'Children were at one time brought to Madron Well to be cured of shingles, wildfires, tetters, and various skin diseases, as well as to fortify them against witchcraft and other mysterious ailments. The child was stripped naked, then it was plunged or popped three times through the water against the sun; next it was passed nine times quickly round the spring going from east to west or with the sun; then dressed, rolled up in something warm, and made to sleep near the water; if the child slept and plenty of bubbles rose in the water, it was a good sign . . .'

And the healing power of Madron Well was not restricted to children. Bishop Hale of Exeter testified that he had seen a man, who had walked on his hands for as long as sixteen years, suddenly restored. The interesting thing too in this case was that the crippled man had been told through a dream experience to wash in Madron Well.

Another favourite Cornish well of mine is at St Clether. This is a lovely wooded parish, with tall banked narrow twisting lanes. St Clether itself lies beyond the old Davidstow Airfield and through it runs the River Inny on its way to join the Tamar.

I came here on an August afternoon, and the sun gave the river a beautiful silvery glint. Rivers are truly among the most graceful things in Nature, giving the landscape vitality and character — which brings us back to the elusive quality of water.

◄Madron Well showing votive offerings in the shape of rags — even cigarette packets — tied to the branches behind.

St Clether Chapel is roughly half a mile from the church, sunk into the side of a hill and set on ground that slopes down to the river. Once inside its four walls you are immediately aware of the stream that runs from the stone-canopied spring outside, through the chapel, under the altar and out into the open again via the south wall. Chapel and well-head are both fifteenth century, but foundations of the chapel are of Celtic origin.

For years this little building lay roofless and in decay. Then in 1895 the Reverend Sabine Baring-Gould directed restoration operations and nine years later the chapel was dedicated. Services are still occasionally held here. The Saint, a son of the Prince of Carmarthen, was driven out of his country by invaders and lived here a great many years, dying 'at an advanced age'. St Clether used the spring as his baptistry. There are in fact two Holy wells. One standing to the north-east of the chapel and the other in the depth of

▼ St Clether Chapel and Well: 'This is a lovely wooded parish . . .' ▶

the outside wall on the south side. The first, it seems, was used as the baptismal well, and from the second Pilgrims drank. Baring-Gould in his *A Book of Cornwall* described the procedure: 'A relic of the Saint was placed in the channel where exposed; the water flowed over it, acquiring miraculous virtues and was drunk at the second well outside the chapel by those who desired healing.' This, of course, was a conscious effort to practise the vision of the holy waters, as recorded in Ezekiel: 'Afterwards he brought me again to the door of the house; and, behold, waters issued out from under the threshold of the house eastwards: for the forefront of the house stood toward the east, and the waters came down from the right side of the house at the south end of the altar.'

It's said that there are more Saints in Cornwall than in Heaven. Maybe, but we've had our share of Sinners too, while the Saints must have been a pretty mixed bunch — as that wit and poet of Penwith, Arthur Caddick, once put it:

> *I am not one of those who'd stoop*
> *To vilify a Cornish Saint —*

St Neot Well: inside are shelves on which butter was cooled.

Most needed baths and some were nuts,
Others, the cuckoo-side of quaint.

For all that, I would like to have met St Neot. Some say he was related to King Alfred which, of course, would make him a Saxon — not Celtic — Saint. Whenever I drive through the village that bears his name, I think of him. St Neot is a big and beautiful parish — the second biggest in all Cornwall — standing on a tributary of the lovely Fowey River, the St Neot River. It's said for a thousand years people have been drawing water from *his* well, and that it's never run dry. St Neot himself stood in it, water up to his neck, reciting the psalms. Like Arthur, though, he is something of a mystery. Disentangling the fact from the fiction is the problem — and the fun.

These then are just three of our Cornish Wells. A journey among them is an admirable way of exploring Cornwall and in visiting them you somehow get in touch with the past, for these wells in spirit have incredibly escaped the march of time.

Some Strange Deaths

Death can be a strange business.

There was an old gentleman, who lived near Bude in North Cornwall, who told some close friends that, one day, he would commit suicide. He was specific too in that he named a certain tree as his place of death. It was a strange little episode because the man wasn't depressed. He had enjoyed his life but, deep down, he felt he was getting old, and the day would surely dawn when he would see no further point in living. Then, suddenly without further warning, he vanished. His friends were certain what had happened — he had kept his word — and just to confirm the matter of his death they went to the tree. But the old gentleman had disappointed them or so it seemed. Then one of the party looked over the hedge and there he was lying on the ground with a broken neck, rope in hand, dead.

At the inquest it was revealed he had died when attempting to tie the rope around a branch of the tree, he had tripped and fallen through the hedge breaking his neck in the process.

Suicide or accident? Either way, it was a strange end.

Murder, too, is often intriguing, especially the motivation. My old friend, Doctor Denis Hocking the well-known pathologist, says: 'The perfect murder is the one that has never been detected . . . the one that nobody knows anything about . . .' A fascinating definition, and, of course, there is frequently a slender thread between conviction and innocence.

The murder of Richard Francis Roadley is a perfect example: the inability of a man to keep his mouth discreetly shut.

Eighty-four-year-old Roadley was a bachelor, wealthy and slightly eccentric. A native of Lincolnshire, where he was Lord of the Manor at Scotter, he had farmed Budds Titson, a farm in the parish of Marhamchurch, for forty years. He had now retired to a four-roomed cottage. Titson is a tiny hamlet, roughly a mile and a half from Marhamchurch village, high on the North Cornish coast.

What the local community knew about Roadley would not have covered the single side of a postcard. A secretive man, he never spoke to anyone about his business affairs. But he was generous: no appeal for a worthwhile cause was ever turned down. His age, his reputed wealth, his recluse-like behaviour and the chaotic conditions in which he lived combined to make him a living legend.

February in North Cornwall can be a tempestuous month. You can expect gales coming off the Atlantic and on occasions the real threat of snow. Nature is not quite stirring from her winter slumbers. Roadley may well have been wide awake that February evening, but he was no longer agile enough or strong enough to defend himself in a desperate situation.

It was a neighbouring farmer, Charles Hicks, living only two hundred yards away, who first suspected that something might be wrong. At 1 p.m. on the Sunday — 19 February 1928 — he noticed that Roadley had not drawn his window blinds — and this was unusual, for the old man had regular habits. Charles Hicks, concerned, entered the cottage and found Roadley lying on his side on the floor of the living room, his head in a pool of blood, the frontal bone of his skull badly fractured. Dr Holtby of Bude was sent for immediately, who, in turn, sent for the police. Roadley died at 7.45 that Sunday evening, and the police, assembling their indictable offence report, classified the death in one word: Murder.

Some notes — £1 and 10s notes — were found near the body. Upstairs a canvas trunk had been cut open and two leather handbags had also been cut open. Drawers in the chest of drawers had been pulled out and ransacked.

The murderer — or murderers — had clearly been in a hurry.

Murder by violence in the Westcountry rarely seems to succeed. Maybe the 'bush telegraph' of our rural areas has something to do with it. In 1854 Llewellin Harvey raped and murdered twenty-one-year old Mary Richards in North Devon. Within a matter of hours the rapist was in custody — in time for Mary to identify him before she died. More recently in the case of the killing of the Falmouth tobacconist on Christmas Eve, the murderer was charged at 10 p.m. on Christmas Day.

But here at Titson the police were groping. The motive was obvious — robbery — but there was no hint as to the identity of the killer. For seven days the crime was a baffling mystery.

However Scotland Yard assistance was requested and the Cornish police began diligently combing the territory for miles around. A tramp, with blood on his clothing, became the number one suspect. But he insisted he had acquired the blood when helping an injured woman from an ambulance at Stratton. The facts were checked — and he was telling the truth.

On Saturday, 25 February, two police officers — in part of the combing exercise — visited a bungalow called Hillside, just off the sloping road below Penfound Manor at Poundstock. Thirty-seven-year old William John Maynard, small-holder and rabbit-trapper, was not at home; but his wife told the policemen where they would find him.

On seeing the two officers, Maynard said immediately: 'I know what you have come about. You have come about that job at Titson.' Within minutes he was perspiring and becoming agitated.

Those two careless sentences were the beginning of the end for Maynard.

Just over three months later Maynard stood trial at the Bodmin Assizes before a packed court. Counsel for the Prosecution was Mr Rayner Goddard, K.C. — later Lord Chief Justice of England.

Maynard accused the police of using strong arm tactics, implicated a local man as 'an accomplice', and then on day two of the trial collapsed during the course of his cross-examination.

Mr Goddard, addressing the all-male jury, submitted that the case had been proved up to the hilt. 'You have before you a statement which experienced officers have sworn was taken from Maynard . . . You will have to judge whether that is a genuine statement. Prisoner does not suggest that it was wrung from him by violent cross-examination, but that it was a fabrication of the police . . . police officers concocted this story, put it down in writing, and then forced him to sign it. If such a thing were to happen it would be good-bye to any confidence in our police in England and to any hope of justice for any accused man.'

On the subject of Maynard's whereabouts on the night of the murder Mr Goddard said: 'If an innocent man had been in his own outhouse, setting traps for work, do you think there is any reason at all for that man to ask another to tell a lie and say "For God's sake tell the police a lie, and tell them I was some place where I was not?" '

Mr Lawrance, replying for the Defence, said: 'First of all

assuming that the jury rejects the idea that Roadley met his death by accident . . . were they sure they had the right man in the dock? Mr Goddard had stated the object of the attack was robbery. He said the prisoner was short of money. That was most unfounded and incorrect.'

Continuing to address the men on the jury, Mr Lawrance said that on the Saturday night Maynard was detained, he had a sleepless night and he was asked to surrender the clothes he was wearing. It was said he volunteered to make another statement. 'Then Pill (Inspector William M. Pill of the Cornwall Constabulary) fetches these skilful detectives from Scotland Yard, with all their capacity and all their Scotland Yard training, and they had him in a room alone, and they take down a statement. I have never understood why a man should not be invited to write down a statement himself if he can write. There was no solicitor present to protect the prisoner; there was no competent friend there to guide or help. He was . . . under the moral pressure, the moral coercion of the presence of two skilful, trained men. He says: "I don't know what I said; I don't remember whether I made a statement."

'Was that unthinkable? They knew that on the next day he was in a prostrate condition.'

Speaking of the blood on his clothes, Mr Lawrance said that Maynard had caught his fingers in a gin. The jury would know that even when they shaved there was a considerable quantity of blood.

'The evidence in the case is circumstantial, and is therefore dependent on inferences. Inferences may be sound or unsound. They are dangerous . . .

'If you have any doubts . . . then this unhappy man is entitled to the benefit of the doubt.'

The jury, in fact, deliberated for forty-five minutes.

Maynard, his arms gripped by two warders, stood in the dock and watched the jury file back into the box in silence.

'Do you find the prisoner Guilty or Not Guilty?'

'Guilty,' came the foreman's reply.

Turning to the motionless Maynard, the clerk said, 'You stand convicted of murder. Have you anything to say why the court should not give you judgement to die, according to law?'

'I am not guilty, my Lord,' replied Maynard in a husky voice.

With the solemn square of black silk placed upon his head, his Lordship passed sentence.

'Amen,' said the chaplain.

Maynard's lips moved, but no words came.

No words came — if Maynard had kept his mouth shut on that Saturday in February he would probably have got away with it.

In the opinion of one police officer: Maynard hanged himself . . . hanged by his own tongue.

Today Titson remains a small, quiet unspoilt hamlet. More than fifty years on, the Roadley murder is still remembered. For the young it has become a piece of misty folklore; for some of the older inhabitants it remains a vivid memory — but a few prefer to leave the murderer and his victim in peace.

Roadley's farm is there. But the thatched cottage in which he died is now only a ruin. I found it by a wooden milk churn stand, almost opposite that austere stone chapel which Roadley himself attended. But you will find no Roadley grave, neither here in the local cemetery nor in Marhamchurch, for his body was taken back to his native Lincolnshire.

Blackberry bushes and brambles spread themselves across what was once the murder room. Standing before this skeleton of a building, framed by trees, I wondered why. What drove Maynard to strike that murderous blow?

In the little road that runs down by the side of the chapel, I leant on a gate and looked across the same fields that Maynard trod that Saturday night on his way home to Hillside.

Did he kill for money? Did he intend to kill at all? Did something go wrong with his plan? Was there an accomplice? Or was there a motive other than robbery? Looking across this quiet green farming landscape I realized those questions can now never be answered.

The ruined cottage retains its secret.

'The Cornishman is fond of private secrets,' the great Cornish painter Peter Lanyon once reflected. 'A solemn intercourse of native with native, often intimate, is mistaken for a gossiping and vicious moralizing. The bush telegraph which puts the GPO to shame is part of this intimate revelation from native to native.'

William Garfield Rowe lived one very private secret for a very long time, and, in a way, died because of it too. The life and death of William Rowe combine to make surely one of the strangest stories Cornwall has known.

For a large portion of his life, he was 'an invisible man'. A deserter from the British Army in the first World War, he became a living lie. To the people of the Porthleven area, William Rowe changed from a young man into just a memory. He detested war, and hid at home in a quite extraordinary fashion; his family running the farm in the daylight hours and only when the sun had truly set in the west did William emerge from his secret room in the house to work. When daylight came back into the landscape William Rowe returned to his hiding place. His was a curious half-world.

For three decades he ceased to exist in the eyes of Cornish society: he was simply another young Cornishman who had not returned from the War — that was the story and the Rowe family stuck to it. Even when his father died and the family moved to Constantine, the incredible mixture of fact and fiction was sustained: William Rowe travelling to his new home Nanjarrow, a remote farm at Constantine, hiding under a hillock of sacks on a cart.

In 1954 his life became more complicated through the death of his brother Stanley. Now Mrs Rowe and her 'invisible' son ran the farm on a shift basis: mother by day, son by darkness. But time was running out for Mrs Rowe: she had only two more years to live and that could have spelt disaster for William. But Fate saved him in the shape of the young Queen Elizabeth, who declared an amnesty for all deserters in both wars. After nearly forty years of 'invisible' living, William Rowe went to the local police station and re-entered life.

But those long years of hiding had turned him into a genuine recluse. He kept very much to himself, and rumours began to circulate to the effect that he was a wealthy man. In 1960, someone robbed £200 from the farm during one of his regular shopping expeditions. Not a great sum of money, but the belief of great wealth still circulated and this being Cornwall speculation, no doubt, added noughts to the figure.

Anyway on the night of 14 August 1963 William Rowe, then aged sixty-four, was brutally murdered at Nanjarrow by two young men. The house was ransacked — robbery being the motive — the two young men walking out with only £2 each, failing to detect £3,000 in the house.

The murderers, Russell Pascoe and Dennis Whitty, were tracked down and sentenced to death. It was to become a classic Cornish murder case: the only double hanging in the long, grisly history of the Bodmin Assizes.

But the strange story doesn't end there.

Police officers at Nanjarrow: 'On the night of 14 August 1963 William Rowe was brutally murdered by two young men.'

Was William Rowe a wealthy man? Or was it all just idle gossip and speculation?

His will revealed a sum of over £8,000 and during the course of the trial at Bodmin there were references to 'thousands of pounds'. The stranger-than-fiction element deepened when it was discovered that, among the murdered man's possessions, was a text book on Esperanto, the international language. William Rowe had written a treasure map, his notes leading to places on the farm. Seekers discovered a big glass jar — inside were hundreds of banknotes, each rolled and pushed through the neck of the bottle. Further clues guided the seekers to a cowshed where a safe was set in concrete, concealed by straw.

But the extent of the 'fortune' remains a true Cornish mystery. The police were not responsible for the recovery of the money. Only those, legally entitled to it, will ever know the true value of William Rowe's 'private banking'. And even they may have got it wrong. Who is not to say that more money lies buried and beyond human reach at Nanjarrow?

A strange man and a perhaps unfinished story.

★ ★ ★ ★ ★

'It has vitality and vulgarity.'

That was Sir John Betjeman writing his thoughts about Newquay back in the 1960s. It still has both those features today.

Newquay was, in fact, the scene of one of the most infuriating jigsaw puzzles in the annals of Westcountry crime — infuriating for the Cornish Police and for one man in particular.

Ex Detective-Superintendent Sydney Roberts 'will remember Friday 11 July 1958 for as long as I live'.

The former Chief of CID in Cornwall talked to me at his home in Porth about the baffling case that became known as 'the Greenshirt murder'. Outside it was a blazing summer day 'like that Friday twenty-three years ago,' reflected Sydney Roberts.

'Mr Horace Hand, a frail 65 year-old retired milk roundsman from Oldham was on the last day of his Cornish holiday. He and his wife were sitting in their car at Towan Headland, Newquay, while his daughter and son-in-law were shopping in the town.

'Shortly after 11.30 Mr Hand decided to go for a stroll. His wife watched him walk slowly over the grass and enter the public

lavatory on the Headland.' She was never to see her husband alive again. Although the lavatory was within sight and sound of hundreds of holidaymakers, inside Mr Hand was viciously attacked. 'Within seconds of the attack, three young men on holiday from the Northcountry entered the lavatory and found a man leaning over Mr Hand who had collapsed into one of the stalls. "This man has had an accident," he explained. "I'll run to a telephone and get an ambulance." The three accepted this suggestion but they soon discovered that the man, wearing a green shirt, had been in the act of robbing Mr Hand. His tobacco pouch and pipe were lying on the floor . . . and lying there too and wrapped inside the pages of *The Daily Mail* of Monday 8 July was a smooth flat stone, a heavy stone though. And the interesting thing was that the *Daily Mail's* front page was missing. Now that front page contained the story of a case I was already working on at Bude. A husband, on his honeymoon, had allegedly pushed his bride over a cliff. He then went down on to the beach and assaulted her about the head with a flat stone. The woman did not die but sustained severe injury. I've always believed that many criminals are copy cats, and the Newquay murderer could have read the paper and thought "This is an idea!"'

'Anyway Mr Hand was rushed to the City Hospital at Truro, but he never regained consciousness. He died at five o'clock that afternoon.

'The telephone exchange at Truro did, in fact, receive a 999 call when a man's voice said "Come quick. There has been an accident." The phone number he gave didn't exist, but we think it was probably a subscriber's call. The caller though was never traced.'

Sydney Roberts explained the immensity of his task and the need for rapid action. 'I travelled to Newquay in a fast car to take charge of operations. It was change-over weekend at Newquay and I knew that the next morning, Saturday, something like 15,000 to 20,000 visitors would have left Newquay and another 15,000 to 20,000 would be on their way in. It was just about one of the worst weekends in the whole year from our angle.

'At least, we had a description of the man. The three holiday-makers from the North had given us that. He was approximately

◄Sydney Roberts, the former Chief of Cornwall CID 'will remember Friday 11 July for as long as I live'.

25, five foot six or seven inches in height, medium to good build, broad shoulders, round face, fair complexion, dark hair greased and brushed back, wearing a green open neck shirt with sleeves rolled up, medium grey trousers.

'But I was working against the clock . . . a single afternoon and a night before the change-over. Police from all parts of Cornwall poured into Newquay and we formed a cordon around the town. All police leave was stopped throughout the county, and those on leave were called back. A complete house-to-house coverage began: hotels, smaller bed-and-breakfast places and private houses.

'Cornwall's biggest manhunt it was . . . we had troops helping us to comb the surrounding countryside and miles of sand dunes. The RAF helped with aerial photography and we had blow-ups of people bathing in the sea near the Headland around the time of the murder or who were simply basking in the sun. That way alone we questioned 149 people.

'In all we distributed questionnaires to well over 4,000 Newquay properties.'

Police, aided by troops and the Civil Defence, scoured the town of Newquay, the beaches and all open spaces. Men in the street, who fitted the description, were challenged on the spot.

'It was a vicious attack,' said Sydney Roberts as we looked at old press photographs of the manhunt. 'If Horace Hand had recovered, I doubt if he would have been able to tell us much. The blow was almost certainly struck from behind. Mr Hand was wearing a trilby yet Dr Hocking, at the post mortem, discovered that he had died from severe head injuries . . . vicious it must have been . . . to have inflicted those injuries through that hat.'

Scotland Yard officers came down to help their Cornish colleagues, and though finger prints and other items went to Scotland Yard for examination the murderer remained elusive.

Cornwall's biggest manhunt and diligent police work both at Newquay and in other parts of the country meant that over 3,000 people were tracked down and made statements about their move-

'Shortly after 11.30 Mr Hand decided to go
for a stroll. His wife watched him walk slowly
over the grass and enter the public lavatory on the
Headland . . . inside Mr Hand was viciously attacked.' ▶

92

ments on that Friday morning. 'But we never had a really strong suspect.

'It was the only unsolved murder in my time as Chief of the Cornish CID,' said Sydney Roberts thoughtfully. 'I am certain robbery was the motive . . . but Mr Hand's holiday money was still tied in a bundle around his neck under his shirt.

'We believe the murderer was on holiday. He was possibly a loner. The change-over must have helped him and the fact that it was a glorious summer's day. On holiday and on such a day, nobody was looking for violence . . .'

In Search of Proof

Proof is a difficult word to define. 'The camera cannot lie' was once accepted as Gospel. But now the idea would be ridiculed. The instances of trick photography have been too numerous for comfort. Even the painting signed by the artist is no guarantee.

Turning to my battered old copy of the *Concise Oxford Dictionary*, I liked 'Evidence sufficing or helping to establish a fact'. Perhaps the most we can hope for in pursuing the subject of this book is proof that 'helps to establish . . .' and, of course, we shall always have the Doubting Thomases. In this chapter we look at 'proof' in two fascinating areas, namely UFOs and the results of healing.

Personally I think a collective sighting of something strange or Supernatural is stronger than say a single person seeing something that may have been a trick of light or some innocent delusion. Here, for example, is a report, published by *The West Briton* on 15 July 1976, relating to an incident on 9 July of that year.

'For about five minutes on Friday, three adults and at least 90 children at Treleigh CP School, Redruth, watched a spherical object cross high in the midday sky . . . and what exactly it was is a complete mystery to them.

'Most of them — they watched from the school yard — agreed that it resembled two dinner plates face to face.

' "It was white and spinning," said Miss Deborah Foster, a teacher. "It appeared to be very high up and came from the Truro direction. We lost sight of it over Carn Brea. It was saucer-shaped and seemed to have an aura or halo."

'Another teacher, Mr Sam Hawkins, said he clearly saw silver and yellow flashes at 90 degrees to the object's direction. He said it was travelling very slowly. "It went through high cloud, yet we could still see it," he added.

'Mrs Sylvia Harris, school secretary, agreed it was round and whitish. She also saw flashes from it. "They were like lightning and were spasmodic," she said. "I have never seen anything like it before."

'Miss Foster added: "It was a little frightening. I do not like anything I cannot explain."

'Pupils said there was no sound, and the sphere changed to a green hue when it went behind high clouds. They agreed it was spinning and they saw flashes from it. They were certain it bore no markings.

'Mr Sidney Thorne, headmaster — who is interested in unidentified flying objects — missed the sighting. He said it could not have been a weather balloon, as the object's journey included a distinct manoeuvre. He added that unexplained objects had been sighted at the school and by parents at Northcountry, Redruth, in March and November, 1973.'

Who can honestly doubt these teachers and pupils saw something that positively defied human explanation? Anyway at this stage in my journey among strange happenings, I decided to positively search for people who could help to establish some facts about healing.

If proof is in the pudding, then in healing proof is surely in the patient.

It is always encouraging to hear when a reader has been genuinely helped. Someone, who I had once known as a very active young sportsman — a fast bowler on the cricket field in summer and a big bustling footballer in the other sporting season — told me how he had been so intrigued by my chapter on Alan Nance in *Supernatural in Cornwall* that he made an appointment.

In telling me his experiences, he preferred to remain anonymous as he felt very critical of the medical profession's attitude. 'Only by going to Harley Street did I convince them that I was suffering very badly from my back. One doctor thought I ought to go to a psychiatrist because I didn't like work! But the Harley Street specialist confirmed I was in real trouble . . . to the extent that I obtained an Industrial Disability Pension.

'Anyway I made this appointment to see Mr Nance at St Austell. Well, one of his lady helpers there put her hands on my spine and said, "You've got a trapped nerve here." That was something nobody in the medical profession had diagnosed and it was something which hadn't shown up in X-rays.

'It was Mr Nance who suggested I should go and see Mr Richards, a bone setter who lives at Penwithick. Well, I can't say that I'm cured . . . but a specialist had told me that if they operated on me I should end up in a wheel chair . . . that was after I'd convinced them I wasn't trying it on!

'So I went to see Mr Richards and he said, "You've got disc trouble." He placed pressure on my back on one particular spot and the relief was enormous. As a result I found myself walking around more easily; able to sit for longer spells in a chair. I may not be cured but a combination of healing and bone setting have given me a lot of help. I'm able to move better and I'm altogether more mobile.

'I may sound as if I'm slating the medical profession but what I'm telling you is the truth. The other interesting thing is that my wife was also suffering from back trouble . . . not as acutely as mine . . . but she saw the improvement in me and decided "I'll have a go too!" And again healing has helped her.

'Perhaps just as interesting is the fact that our dog has responded to healing. She's a good housedog . . . quite an aggressive character really . . . but when we took her into this room where they do the healing at Mr Nance's her personality changed. She became a much more placid dog . . . became quite a different dog in fact . . . responding to the very peaceful atmosphere down there.'

One of the finest advertisements for spiritual healing I have had the good luck to meet was Danny Warren, then a fifteen-year-old schoolboy living at St Austell. Danny had been born with a hole in his heart. The medical profession declined to consider an operation and his mother was told 'Better to have a son 50 per cent alive than 100 per cent dead!'

Danny's father recalled taking him out to play ball on the green. 'Danny used to come in after five minutes, finished. He'd just stretch out, his face like a brandy bottle, at times he'd go purple.'

Then Alan Nance started giving Danny spiritual healing at the age of nine. Within a matter of two months there was a vast improvement in Danny's physical shape and approach to life — to such an extent that when I met him as a fifteen-year-old he was playing cricket and soccer, riding a cycle and swimming. In the young man's own words: 'It's a different life altogether. I can remember the heat when Mr Nance laid hands on me . . . like two hot water bottles.'

Danny is now living in Canada and Alan Nance hears from him, usually at Christmas time. Alan Nance recalled: 'I had one snippet of interesting information with his 1979 card. Danny wrote: "As a point of interest I had a medical check-up a few weeks ago, and the doctor wouldn't believe I ever had a hole in the heart . . . but we know, don't we?" '

Knowing that I was keen to learn about people who had been helped through healing, Alan Nance was able to produce these two testimonies. 'They're very typical,' he explained, 'just two of many cases.'

The first, from David Chappell of St Austell, read: 'For over twenty years I suffered with my back, having curvature of the spine and at times being in great pain. Having had treatment from doctors, hospital and an osteopath I went to see Mr Nance, being recommended to him by an acquaintance, and after a number of visits I found the pain in my back was considerably easier. This was over two years ago and since then I have had no serious trouble.'

While W.L. Jones gratefully wrote: 'I had suffered from severe arthritis of both hips since February 1978. I started visiting Mr Nance in June 1978 with the aid of two sticks and pain killers. After a few weeks I found the pain much relieved. I had a hip replacement operation in October 1978 and afterwards continued my healing with Mr Nance. Today I can walk unaided and without the use of pain killers.'

Then a third testimony came from Ann Fitzpatrick of Lanivet. 'Ever since I was seven years old, I have suffered from psoriasis . . . all over my body, especially my arms and leg . . . which has made me very embarrassed when in company.

I have been to several doctors and specialists and had been treated with various cures, none of which helped at all. Then I heard of Mr Nance and his healing powers. So in February 1979 I attended my first session and by August of that year I was able to wear for the first time . . . without embarrassment . . . short-sleeved tops and dresses. I am now 70 years of age . . . and, oh, I wish I had tried faith healing before.'

One of Alan Nance's particularly happy recollections concerns Amanda who was six years old at the time.

'On 26 November 1980, her father called on me at 2.30 p.m., and told me that Amanda was having a bad attack of asthma. Her doctor said that if she was not better by 5 p.m. then she was to go

98

into hospital. Her father naturally hoped that healing would make this unnecessary. I went with him arriving at their home at about 2.45. Amanda was in a very distressed condition due to the difficulty in breathing.

'I laid hands on her and her breathing gradually improved. In about half an hour she was lifting her head and smiling at her father. After lifting my hands from her, she lay back. But after about fifteen minutes the asthma was obviously building up again, her breathing was quickening and she was nervously picking at her lip. I took her hand and smoothing down her hair, I whispered reassuring and comforting words to her. The stress gradually began to be lifted and her breathing returned to normal.

'I left at 4 p.m., saying that if her father was in any way doubtful when I finished my healing clinic, he was to come for me again. However he telephoned me at 6.30 p.m. explaining she was now greatly improved and was having her tea! There was no renewal of the condition and she has been all right since.'

Another reader, who was encouraged to try spiritual healing, was Donald Hunt, a retired mining engineer living at Fowey. Admittedly, Donald Hunt had been helped enormously through healing at an earlier point in his life, as he told me when he came to see us at Land's End cottage one afternoon.

'In 1935 I was hit in the right eye by a rubber band and spent two weeks in Westminster Hospital,' he told me. 'Medical diagnosis was "Blood in the Anterior Chamber and Endo-dialyses", that is two small holes piercing the eye at the lower edge of the iris and blinding by internal bleeding. The bleeding stopped and the blood in the eye was slowly absorbed, thus restoring vision, but the holes remained and acted like "pin-hole cameras". As a result triple vision was experienced — one normal image plus two others higher up. This interfered with tennis and other sporting activities. Two opthalmic surgeons were consulted and both stated that nothing could be done, as this type of injury had never been known to heal.

'At this time I heard of a Spiritualist healer living in South Tottenham and made an appointment to see him. He was a signalman employed by the LMSR and lived in a very well-kept terrace house. I examined him closely on our way upstairs to the small, simply furnished room in which he did his healing. He was a short slightly-built man in his late fifties or early sixties and spoke in a rather uneducated voice using a simple vocabulary. The window of the room was blacked out but good illumination was provided by a strong red bulb in a standard lamp.

'The healer went into trance and although watched most carefully showed no sign that this was faked. His eyes remained firmly closed and his movements were unhesitating and accurate. His voice now became much deeper, but unstrained, and he spoke very good English employing an extensive vocabulary with a slight foreign accent. He purported to have been a North American Indian.

'I was asked to hold my hands in front of me, palms uppermost and with no hesitation he placed his own hands, palms down, about half-an-inch above them . . . how did he know exactly where my hands were? After three or four seconds he described my eye injury accurately, in both medical and non-medical terms, and also how it had occurred.

'Eye injuries, he said, were difficult to heal and he made no promises, but thought that, with patience, something might be done. Treatment was given by holding one hand behind and close to my head and the other close to and in front of the injured eye. Tingling and heat were experienced and also a sharp pricking sensation in the eye itself.

'Treatment continued twice weekly for about eighteen months by which time vision had become normal although the eye tended to be easily dazzled by bright lights. No payment was asked but contributions could be placed in collecting boxes for well-known charities — this was entirely voluntary.

'In the autumn of 1940 I was passed as "fit for aircrew" by a RAF Medical Board. The eye was examined for a long time and I was told that it was unheard of for an eye injury, of the type I had sustained, to heal. It was examined out of interest by medical practitioners in all departments as well as the opthalmic surgeons whose concern it was.'

In the light of that kind of experience only a fool would place limits on the power of healing.

ACKNOWLEDGEMENTS

I am especially indebted to all the people who have given me interviews for this book, and allowed me to quote them — also to Mr Knight and Mrs Olds at the Local Studies Department of the Cornwall County Library at Redruth.

In addition my special thanks to the following: to Brenda Duxbury for editing this and all our Bossiney titles, Joy Francis for help in research and typing, Kay Isbell, who is the model for our cover — once more Ray Bishop has produced a first-class cover and illustrations — Charles Woolf for supplying some splendid photographs, Denis Mitchell for the Alfred Wallis illustration and Andrew Lanyon for the postcard of Wallis's store at St Ives. And, of course, to my wife Sonia and secretary Janet Down, who have been about other Bossiney business, while I have been writing this my tenth title — and enabling me to start on no. 11.

ALSO AVAILABLE

CORNISH MYSTERIES

by Michael Williams. 40 photographs.
Cornish Mysteries is a kind of jig-saw puzzle in words and pictures. The power of charming, mysterious shapes in the Cornish landscape, the baffling murder case of Mrs Hearn are just some fascinating ingredients.
'... superstitions, dreams, murder, Lyonesse, the legendary visit of the boy Jesus to Cornwall, and much else. Splendid, and sometimes eerie, chapters.'

The Methodist Recorder

SUPERNATURAL IN CORNWALL

by Michael Williams. 24 photographs.
'... a book of fact, not fiction ... covers not only apparitions and things that go bump in the night, but also witchcraft, clairvoyancy, spiritual healing, even wart charming ...'

Jenny Myerscough on BBC

'Serious students of ghost-hunting will find a fund of locations.'

Graham Danton on Westward TV

OCCULT IN THE WEST

by Michael Williams. Over 30 photographs. Price
Michael Williams follows his successful *Supernatural in Cornwall* with further interviews and investigations into the Occult — this time incorporating Devon. Ghosts and clairvoyancy, dreams and psychic painting, healing and hypnosis are only some of the facets of a fascinating story.
'... provides the doubters with much food for thought.'

Jean Kenzie, Tavistock Gazette

KING ARTHUR COUNTRY in CORNWALL, THE SEARCH for the REAL ARTHUR

by Brenda Duxbury, Michael Williams and Colin Wilson.
Over 50 photographs and 3 maps.
An exciting exploration of the Arthurian sites in Cornwall and Scilly, including the related legends of Tristan and Iseult, with The Search for the Real Arthur by Colin Wilson.
'... provides a refreshing slant on an old story linking it with the present.'

Caroline Righton. The Packet Newspapers

LEGENDS OF CORNWALL

by Sally Jones. 60 photographs and drawings.
Brilliantly illustrated with photographs and vivid drawings of legendary characters. A journey through the legendary sites of Cornwall, beginning at the Tamar and ending at Land's End.
'Highly readable and beautifully romantic ...'

Desmond Lyons, Cornwall Courier

OTHER BOSSINEY TITLES INCLUDE

CASTLES OF CORNWALL
by Mary and Hal Price

DISCOVERING BODMIN MOOR
by E.V. Thompson

GATEWAY TO CORNWALL
by Joan Rendell

FOLLOWING THE TAMAR
by Sarah Foot

VIEWS OF OLD CORNWALL
by Sarah Foot

MY CORNWALL

FOLLOWING THE RIVER FOWEY
by Sarah Foot

POLDARK COUNTRY
by David Clarke

MAKING POLDARK
by Robin Ellis

THE CRUEL CORNISH SEA
by David Mudd

AROUND HELSTON & LIZARD
with Sheila Tracy

HOME ALONG FALMOUTH AND PENRYN
by David Mudd

AROUND & ABOUT THE ROSELAND
by David Mudd

ALONG THE BUDE CANAL
by Joan Rendell

ABOUT MEVAGISSEY
by Brenda Duxbury

ALONG THE CAMEL
by Brenda Duxbury & Michael Williams

ABOUT ST JUST IN PENWITH
by Frank Ruhrmund

ABOUT THE CITY A PORTRAIT OF TRURO
by David Mudd

THE LIZARD
by Jill Newton

THE FALMOUTH PACKETS
by David Mudd

PENZANCE TO LAND'S END
by Michael Williams

MY GRANDFATHER ISAAC FOOT
by Sarah Foot

ABOUT LOOE
by Brenda Duxbury

CORNWALL & SCILLY PECULIAR
by David Mudd

We shall be pleased to send you our catalogue giving details of our growing list of titles for Devon and Cornwall and forthcoming publications.

If you have difficulty in obtaining our titles, write directly to Bossiney Books, Land's End, St Teath, Bodmin, Cornwall.